THE BEST H.E.L.P.

(HOLISTIC EXAMPLES OF LEARNED PRACTICE)

BOOK

Helping Children

And Young People

To Reach Their Full Potential

BY KEMI FOLARIN

The Best H.E.L.P Book (Holistic Examples Of Learned Practice)

Copyright © 2017 by Young People Matter publisher

The old Laundry 20 Eastcote street Stockwell SW9 9BY

www.youngpeoplematter.org

www.kemifolarin.com

ISBN 978-0-9957115-0-1 (Paperback Edition)

Edited by Joanna Oliver

Front cover by bassetown.com

First Printed in the United Kingdom June 2017

ACKNOWLEDGEMENTS

I dedicate The BEST H.E.L.P. Book to my dad, Femi Folarin, who sadly passed away in 2014. I love you dearly and know that you are watching over me. To my wonderful mum, who showed me by her actions the value of hard work, love and kindness. To my mentors, Tolu Oyerinda, Joanna Oliver and close friends who believed in me even when I did not. To my young people, who have allowed me to be part of their journey; you have kept me going through the hard times, because you are the reason I do what I do. Finally, thank you to my creator for giving me life and a purpose on earth. God blessed me with such gifts with which to bless the world.

CONTENTS

FOREWORD

It is hard to believe how much time has flown since I first met Kemi. I remember her always being busy zipping between Uni classes in Kingston and a youth work job she had in the idyllic Ham & Petersham area of Richmond Upon Thames known for its historic meadows and internationally prized gardens; a far cry from our shared and beloved, South London.

We met in Brixton in 2006, 10 years after Tony Blair's famous five pledges—he promised his New Labour government would deliver on cutting class sizes down to 30 or under and introduced fast track punishment for persistent young offenders. My son Quinntin was four years old at the time and the conversations I had with Kemi then were all about how we could, if not create something better, then at least lessen the traumas of being young and growing up in South London. It was a South London that seemed determined to affirm its reputation as the "bad boy" of London, listed as one of the top 10 Dangerous Places to Live in the London. The media was at the beginning of it's now insatiable fixation with gangsterism; mind you, this was still two years before the Metropolitan Police announced that a hand-picked team of elite firearms officers, armed with submachine guns would begin patrolling the streets of London, for the first time in history.

Snapchat wasn't born yet, Kid's Company were handing out Christmas gifts, Operation Trident hadn't been formed, Mark Duggan was 24, and 175 mothers of teenage homicide victims hadn't had to mourn their children yet; things seemed manageable but there were still enough growing instances of fatal and near fatal stabbings and shootings for us all to be concerned. Coming from growing up in New York City, I noticed the same alarming pattern of self-destruction that riddled my own youth—it saddened me deeply. We all seemed to be asking the questions, "Why?" and "How?"

I had a pretty successful music project at the time, TGSMP Music, yet somehow found myself drifting away from the spotlights of mainstream music: MTV, Channel U, 1Xtra, main stages at the O2, Shepherd's Bush Empire, and Brixton Academy and moving more towards youth and community centres throughout the UK. Organisations like the Met Black Police Ass., The Prince's Trust, YMCA, and VH1 were all vying for my attention, yet were failing to act; and while they continued to ask the important questions, Kemi was actually ready to do something, and that she did.

Aged 22, armed with a degree in psychology & sociology, Kemi did do something. She set up and has continued to run a successful, life-saving, intuitive opportunity for children and young people, an opportunity that started from one small funding form and has grown into the multi-award winning Young People Matter Charity – a dedicated community anchor running breakfast and after school clubs, half term and summer play schemes, intergenerational (youth and seniors) projects and programs for families, lone parents and East African women; as well as the Aspire to Elevate social enterprise training centre, offering intensive individual support in gaining adult qualifications.

With over 10 years' experience working in our beloved Borough of Lambeth, Kemi is an unsung hero who has weathered the storm. As a charity director, Kemi has lived through and learnt first-hand the problems young people face, and with this book, she interviews other professionals, experts and industry leaders to contribute their findings alongside her own. The voices of youth and families echo throughout.

Kind regards,
Marcus "Paradise" Dawes
'YPM' Senior Project Co-ordinator

PREFACE

A snap shot of 14 plus years in the field of youth work and play.

8 years old, lining up my teddy bears and dolls preparing them for a class with Kemi, was normal in my household. As a child, my dream was to become a teacher, I would teach my teddies and dolls many things. I was in love with the role of teaching others, from a young age. Fast forward to one sunny day in May, while preparing for my exams at secondary school, I remember going up to the board to write. Once I had completed writing, my teacher looked up and said look at the word 'girl', is there anything wrong with it? I looked and said, 'no Sir' but to my surprise I had written 'grill' instead of 'girl'. This was my first encounter with the word 'Dyslexia'. Sir said, 'you may have dyslexia Kemi' and he went on to explain.

The process began for me, in discovering that I had dyslexia, many thoughts flooded my mind and there were many mixed emotions for me. During my first in-house dyslexia test at college, I was offered extra time in exams but I never used it, out of fear of appearing dumb. This was followed by my second test with a psychologist, in my first year of University. It was confirmed I had mild dyslexia and my dream of become a teacher was looking impossible in my eyes. How was I going to mark student's work, when my own spelling was bad?

From the age of 16 years, my dream of becoming a teacher was firmly out of the picture. Why? Because I allowed my dyslexia to determine the course I could and could not take, from that point forward. I started University, studying Psychology and Sociology and whilst living in Kingston, I saw a job advert for working with children in a holiday camp and I went for it. I knew my dreams of becoming a teacher were put aside but I was still going to be able to work with children. It was a 'Win, win' I thought to myself. My journey working with children and young people started from there at the sweet age of 18, I worked in holiday camps, a Youth Offending Team, did club-based youth work, detached youth work, you name it, I did it.

In 2007, after leaving University aged 22 years, I started a charity called 'Young People Matter', with an aim to help children and young people reach their full potential. My passion was to offer young people all the things that I saw were missing from youth clubs, from my experience and according to the views of the young people I worked with at the time. Throughout my three years at University, I had a book full of worksheets and ideas of activities to do with young people – I still have the book today.

Let me fast forward to 2013, surprisingly I qualified as a teacher in long life learning and opened a training centre, teaching and marking work. Yes, me - I teach and mark work! The day I qualified, it was a wonderful feeling and guess what? I do spot spelling mistakes!

A great lesson I learned from this experience was to not define myself by what I cannot do or by my current situation. After starting my journey into youth work at the age of seventeen, some fourteen and a half years later, I have gathered a vast amount of knowledge and gained a wealth of experience in working with children and young people, a quick snap shot of my key learning over the years include the following points:

- Understanding the importance of first getting to know a young person before trying to help them. Key Note: one size does not fit all.

- The importance of making a young person feel valued and wanted. We all want to feel valued and to know that we belong.

- To not judge a book by its cover, every person on this earth has a story to tell.

- To win a young person's heart, start by caring about what interests them. It's a great feeling when people value or take an interest in your interests, don't you think?

- Early intervention is extremely important, in supporting with breaking the cycles and making a difference for the next generation, whilst providing better opportunities and path ways.

- There are many benefits to offering new opportunities and experiences to young people, in terms of a change in perspectives and being exposed to new things.

- Always keep to your word! Do not promise things you cannot deliver (as it breaks trust).

- Parent and school involvement and contribution amounts to a POWERFULLY holistic way to work with young people.

The following pages of this book were written with the purpose of taking action; taking a stand on behalf of young people, our next generation. We cannot just talk anymore, when youth are dying and I do not just mean physically but also mentally. Together we can make a difference, we can move mountains to help give a better view point. You and I can be the change makers for the next generation.

#THINGSWILLCHANGE

#TAKEASTANDWITHME

INTRODUCTION TO THE BEST H.E.L.P. BOOK

I have often wondered why some people achieve in life and others don't Why do some young people reach their full potential, whilst others do not? Why do some young people join gangs? Why are some young people promiscuous, drug dealers, school drop outs or teenage parents? Why do some young people suffer with mental health issues, such as depression, or have low self-worth? Have these thoughts ever crossed your mind? There are many whys and often we are left without answers or a long-term strategy to tackle these issues. I want to explore what are the secrets or principles for helping young people to achieve?

Late 2013, I determined to find out and share what is the difference that will make the difference in the field of youth work. This led me on a quest for understanding, knowledge and good practice founded on the suggestions and experiences of parents, teachers, youth workers, funders, commissioning officers, MPs and young people. It was a journey which led to the composition of THE BEST H.E.L.P. BOOK, an acronym which stands for holistic examples of learned practice. This book will provide tools, stories and solutions for helping children and young people to flourish.

Amazing work takes place every day across the world and there is learning that can be taken from others' work. This book will share the great work happening and provide tools that can be used to help young people.

The cost of change is often at the forefront of our minds but a question to ask is 'what will be the cost, if things stay the same with our young people?' One person or one group does not hold all the answers but together, the answers will be evident and clear for what it will take to help children and young people reach their full potential. Some tools in this book may be new to you, while others you may already use and even so, this offers an opportunity to reflect upon them, from a different perspective or simply a reminder of the benefits of your approaches. There is always a need for new strategies, new understandings or new tools in this ever-changing world.

There are a range of areas that could have been further explored in this book but have been omitted, perhaps for a later date, such as:

- Criminal Justice system.

- Health and wellbeing.

- Government and law enforcement.

- Disabilities.

- Labelling of children and young people.

However, the areas that were included are based on my experience of working with young people and the views of those interviewed, which provides information to form the foundations for helping children and young people to achieve.

Each chapter draws upon contributions from those interviewed, refers to books and research papers and begins with a story. The goal of this book is to provide tools, solutions and practical activities that can be used to help young people to achieve. Most importantly, my aim is to inspire us all to believe that anything is possible, that we can together make a change in the life of the children and young people we encounter.

By reading this book you may want to achieve one or a selection of the following:

A.   Learn a new skill.

B.   Have a new tool to try.

C.   Improve your communication with young people.

D.   Work with young people in a more holistic way.

E.   All of the above.

Hashtags

Alongside a range of hashtags (#) throughout the book, each chapter incorporates a thinking moment and concludes with reference to a practice tool that you can try. Although this is not presented as a manual, change happens by action, so let us actively begin or continue to bring about a change for children and young people. Please join me in spreading the word about The Best H.E.L.P. book by using **#thebesthelpbook**, or using any of the other hashtags that you see throughout this book, on your social media pages. Why not give it a try, the next time you use social media, hashtag something you have taken from the book.

Before you start reading the Best H.E.L.P. Book I would like to get your creative mind flowing, this book is about solutions and tools to bring about change. So please take part in the activity below before continuing reading.

I want you to think of a minimum of 15 reasons why you believe, some young people are not reaching their full potential.

1.	6.	11.
2.	7.	12.
3.	8.	13.
4.	9.	14.
5.	10.	15.

Now take one of your answers and come up with five ways or actions to take that will aid with overcoming the reason you have suggested.

For example:

Reason: There are not many opportunities for young people.

1. Find out what young people in your local area would like to do, if there were no restrictions.

2. Look for different opportunities on offer from other groups in the area.

3. Apply for funding to be able to offer young people new opportunities.

Reason Chosen:____

Action Steps

1.

2.

3.

4.

5.

Now it is time to take action to help address the problem and help children and young people to reach their full potential.

 # YoungPeopleReallyDoMatter!

Potential Lies Within Us All

"To every problem there is already a solution, whether you know what it is or not"

Grenville Kleiser

Potential lies within us all. Sam was a young man from John Hill estate in South London. Sam along with his three brothers, were a well-known family on the estate and every day was the same for Sam. The ringing of police sirens in his ears, the flashing blue lights through the window, reflecting onto the back of the kitchen wall, meant that he always knew when something was going down outside. His estate was surrounded by tall buildings, that lead to a dark alleyway and Sam had to walk through the alley every day to get to his front door. There were always groups of boys, just sitting on the corner, the air filled with the smell of weed and laughter. This was where Sam lived, the place he called home, the stomping ground where he spent most of his time with friends, it was where he learned about life.

From the age of 16 years, Brixton prison was where Sam spent most of his time, for drug dealing and possession of a fire arm. After several years in and out of prison, during his last sentence for armed robbery, Sam met George, a fellow inmate. Meeting George was the best thing that could have happened to Sam. Despite being inside himself, he was able to help Sam change his outlook on life. George was spending the rest of his life behind bars but was mentally free. He showed Sam how to turn his hustling skills into a business and the importance of the application of knowledge through reading. Sam read every book on business and personal development he could lay his hands on, during his last sentence.

George inspired Sam, in such a way no one had before. He believed in him. After many years behind bars, Sam was ready to face the world, still Sam but with a different mind-set and perspective on life. The gates were pulled open and Sam was a free man. Looking back at the gates he smiled, thinking 'I will never return again'. Sam had a goal and was determined to achieve it, this time round. From a young age, Sam always dreamed of being part of the corporate world; climbing the ladder to the top, becoming a senior manager or CEO of a company, wearing the best designer clothes and tailored suits, posing with bottles in the club, in VIP lounges and owning sports cars, 'living the dream', as it were. Two years on the straight and narrow, Sam's dream of being a business man was becoming a reality. George was happy to pick up the newspaper on Sunday 11th May, because to his surprise Sam's face was on page four. Growing up, Sam's name had always been associated with crime, gang violence and Brixton prison but this time it was associated with positivity.

Sam's belief was that growing up where he did, dreams were just that - dreams - and meant nothing. You had to do what was needed to make money to survive, regardless of what that might be. Perhaps, if he had been raised in a different area, or made better choices in life, he would have focused more on turning his dreams into a reality, rather than falling into a life of crime and easy money. In Sam's eyes, he was successful at what he did, just not the world's definition of successful. Sam did not have the greatest start in life, however his drug selling showed him:

1. How to get customers and keep them.

2. How to buy and sell.

3. How to grow from a one-man team to recruiting new workers to become part of his team.

4. How to generate a lot from a little.

George showed Sam how to use his skills in a better way. Everything that Sam experienced was not a waste, as George showed him how to transfer his skills for drug selling into skills for running a business. Despite his choices in life and the paths previously chosen, his potential and talents never left him, he was like a seed just waiting for the right environment to flourish. For a tree to grow successfully, there are a few key factors needed, right? For some young people, they just need the right environment, opportunities and support, in order to overcome barriers and abandon their old way of living to embark on a new journey.

All young people have potential; some are unaware of their potential while others are aware. I champion what author and speaker, Les Brown proclaims, that "Most people fail in life not because they aim too high and miss but because they aim too low and hit". Sam accomplished great things in his life. George taking the time out to invest and listen to Sam, made a difference. The title of this chapter is 'potential lies within us all' and Sam was discovering his. The time George spent getting to know Sam allowed him to see the potential rather than judging him only by his behaviour or what he had been able to achieve to date. Getting to know a young person before trying to help them is vital in the process of helping children and young people to reach their full potential. Just ask Sam.

Thinking Moment?

Food For Thought: What can you do to help a young person to tap into their potential?

POTENTIAL COVERED IN CLAY

Author and Pastor, Dr Myles Munroe, once preached: "Inside every seed is a tree and the potential from that seed can come a forest". One day a group of people tried to move a statue; whilst moving the statue, it fell and a crack opened, revealing beneath the clay, a gold object and to their surprise, there was a Buddha made of gold. Who would have known beneath the clay was a gold Buddha? Wipe away the surface and see what you discover, better said, look beyond what a person shows you, to discover the true them. Many individuals can be likened to the gold Buddha; they have potential in them just waiting to be discovered. Inside all of us lies the potential to be great, to be amazing.

#Question – Are you able to see the apple in the seed?

The Teenage Years – Adolescence.

Adolescence is a challenging life stage, one we all have or will experience. Coleman and Hendry studied adolescence, in their book 'The Nature of Adolescence' and highlighted the different stages of development that takes place during adolescence, such as changes in the body, the development of morals and values, brain development, emotional development and more. Additionally, a young person starts to develop an identity away from their parents. Adolescence is not an easy stage or time, especially for those from broken homes. A smooth transition into adolescence offers many benefits for the individual, as well as their environment.

We do not have control over the families that we are born into, nor the environments in which we are raised. Author and speaker, John Maxwell states: "Your attitude has a profound influence on how you see the world – and thus on the way you live out your life". Adolescence is a time where young people start to experience the world for themselves, searching for their place and role. D.M Fergusson, L. John Horwood and Elizabeth M. Ridder, found correlations between problems in childhood and later on in life, asserting that many lifelong health behaviours are set during adolescence. Development is generally cumulative, so earlier stages will influence later ones. The way a person chooses to interpret their experiences, will determine how they live their lives. How many people do you know, who define themselves based on how others see them or based on their experiences in life? It is important to educate young people to know in their hearts and minds that they are more than their experiences and achievements. Young people are more then what they do.

I Am More Than My Behaviour.

Before I get started, I want to remind you that greatness lies within every single child you will come into contact with. It is mine and your abilities, experiences and skills that will support young people in unlocking that potential. Everything that we do in life is either to get love or to compensate for lack of love, according to author, Brian

Tracy. There are many different factors affecting children and young people, so many that an entire book can be dedicated to them. It is paramount to look at young people, not in isolation but in a holistic way, exploring social, economic and environmental factors. No one lives on an island alone; therefore, our surroundings will have an effect on us, whether positive or negative. The home should be the foundation of learning, however as social creatures, we also learn from our surrounding environment and experiences with others outside the home.

Activity Time

Make a list of five individuals that you work with or may know, that are deemed 'hard to reach' or not currently achieving. I would like you to look beyond what they tell or show you and seek the greatness inside of them. Pick one out of the five you have selected and list ten great skills, qualities and talents that you observe in them. Now your call to action, see the potential that is yet to come to pass and help that individual to make it happen.

Name of person ______________________________________

Skills, Qualities And Talents

1.

2.

3.

4.

5.

6.

7.

8.

9.

10.

KEEPING GOOD COMPANY

The environment in which a person finds themselves, can shape and influence them. There are hundreds of books available related to 'success' and one common statement found in many of these books is 'Keeping good company'. These books often encourage people to develop mastermind groups, to help them on their path to success. Why? Because we learn daily from our environments, the people we interact with and our experiences.

Young people often copy what they see, as people are influenced by what they see around them. In "Today Matters", John Maxwell refers to an experiment, which illustrates the power of influence. The story centres around a group of monkeys locked in a room and in the middle of the room was a pole with a bunch of bananas at the top. A monkey would climb the pole in hope of reaching the bananas but would be knocked off by a blast of water from a hose. Each time a monkey climbed the pole, it would repeatedly be knocked off - again, again and again. Eventually, the monkeys learned that the climb was hopeless and they would not reach the bananas.

As part of the experiment, new monkeys were placed in the room with a few old ones. The new monkeys would try to climb the pole to reach the banana, however the old monkeys would pull them down, knowing that they too would be blasted with water. One by one, each old monkey was replaced with a new monkey and the same thing happened - a new monkey would try to climb the pole but the old monkeys would pull them down for fear of being blasted - until there were no old monkeys left in the room, with experience of the hose. Nonetheless, none of the new monkeys were allowed to climb, as the other, newer monkeys pulled them down. Not one monkey in the room knew why but none attempted to get the bananas.

#BadCompanycorruptsgoodcharacter.

WHAT IS YOUR PERCEPTION?

What do young people learn from you, by the way you conduct yourself or deal with situations at work or at home? Despite a young person's upbringing, their perception of an experience will influence their behaviour. Let me illustrate this point with a story. A group of people went to war and after fighting furiously; they found themselves in thick woods and soon became surrounded by the opposing side. The General of the troops looked around; they were surrounded from the front and the back, the left and the right, with enemies circling them. The General looked up, "troops", he said boldly, "Well, we are surrounded but at least they can't get away this time!" Perhaps in his opinion, seeing where everyone was gave his troops an advantage.

What a great perspective to have in a potentially troublesome situation. A situation is only as bad as an individual perceives it to be, if one perceives a situation as if there is no way out, they are likely to not look for solutions or to see opportunities. The mind is a powerful tool and controls everything that we do. Inspirational speaker and author, Zig Ziglar once said, "Positive thinking won't allow you to do anything, but will let you to do everything better than negative thinking would." Negative thinking about life will not produce the results a person truly desires but unfortunately, many people become stuck in this way of thinking, while holding onto a dream that appears to be unreal. How you view yourself will determine how you view the potential that lies within you.

Food For Thought: You can't think your way out of a problem but you can think of solutions to help you out of them.

More To Youth Clubs.

During his interview, Anthony Douglas, consultant and manager in the music and acting industry, used a famous quote to sum up the point he was trying to make: "The devil makes work for idol hands". He went on to say that young people do not have many opportunities like they did back in 'his days'. "Back in my days, I remember a number of youth clubs and play centres available in South London. Places for young people to go, relax with friends, learn new skills, play games such as table tennis or football, or other activities such as cooking, or even drama and dance. Due to the decline and absence of services and opportunities available for young people, it is likely that many young people will resort to hanging around on the streets, where the occurrence of criminal activity is very high".

The closure of youth clubs over the last few years, due to funding cuts, has reduced access to centres that were at the heart of many communities. With reductions in youth provision and the rise in gun and knife crime, teenage pregnancy and anti-social behaviour, to name a few things, who is going to fill the gap? The theory of 'doing more with less' is required more than ever in the current climate. Youth centres are a critical element in the process to helping young people to reach their full potential. I will explore the role of youth clubs in more depth in chapter seven.

Food For Thought: One man cannot change the world but together we can work at it!

Wrapping Up Time

Young people are the next generation, our leaders of tomorrow. A minority of young people are making headline news, for all the wrong reasons, being portrayed negatively, judged and criminalized. Failure to address issues affecting young people, especially those who are vulnerable, will evidently cost the economy but most importantly could have lasting negative effects throughout their lives. Although this is with reference to the minority, there are many factors to take into consideration, as to why a person chooses a negative path. However, what is clear, is that their surroundings, environment and home are key places to explore first. The great news is that change is always possible because potential lies within us all.

#Seekforunderstandingandyoushallfindit.

#1 Time To Ask Yourself, What Can I do? – Based upon the premise of people having an inherent need to feel wanted and to belong, ask yourself: 'what can I do right now to help just one young person feel valued on a daily basis?'

Below are a few simple actions, which can be used daily. Why not give it a go today!

Check out John Maxwell's book '25 ways to win with people'.

1.   Listen and show an interest in what a young person is saying.

2.   Remembering what you have been told or heard.

3.   Ask questions.

4.   Give a person an opportunity which they could not give themselves.

5.   Give a compliment within the first three minutes of meeting them.

6.   Smile when you see them.

7.   Remember their name (this really makes a difference).

8.   See everyone as having potential; see him or her as *gold*.

9.   Do not just take things at face value but search for meaning.

   Seek the WHY.

10. Be genuine.

Family Is At The Heart Of It All

"Behind every child who believes in himself is a parent who believed first."

Mathew Jacobson

Billy was a smart little boy and everyone loved him. Billy's nick name was 'hungry Billy' because he was so skinny but loved to eat and never put on any weight. Billy could eat a person out of house and home. Let me share Billy's story.

The odour of sweet smelling bread coming from the kitchen never failed to wake me up every Monday morning. My mum loved to bake and every morning, mum would prepare breakfast for the family. Monday was mum's baking day and she always made enough sweet bread to last the week. The sweet smell was my alarm clock and as soon as I smelled the bread, I would jump up and run to the kitchen.

Mum would be standing there, with the biggest smile on her face, making tea for dad and Kitty, my sister.

When it comes to food, we had one rule in our house; we had to have the first meal of the day together. What's that saying? 'A family that prays together, stays together'? In our home, it was 'a family that eats together, grows together'. Everyone knew that the first slice of the bread was mine, served with freshly squeezed orange juice and setting me up for the day ahead. After breakfast, it was time to get ready for school and before running out of the house to catch my bus, mum would kiss me on my forehead, "Have a lovely day son, now remember mummy loves you" and dad would shout from the kitchen "That's my boy, have a great day".

I had the best mum in the world.......in my dreams. If only my family was really like this.........

My reality was so different. Off goes my alarm, waking me from my lovely dream of fresh bread, baked by a loving mum. First thing in the morning, all I can hear is the pumping of music coming from my sister's room. All I desire at this point, is to be able to go back to sleep, even if it was for only five minutes longer. As I drag myself out of bed, making my way to the kitchen, partly sleep walking, I open the fridge and reach for the milk.

"Damn! The milk is off again" I shout, slamming the milk on the table, mum has not done any shopping, again! For the fourth time this month, I go off to school without breakfast. My family did not have much money; mum could not hold down a job, so she would leave me whatever money she could. One pound was what I got most days for lunch. Now you know how much food that can buy! The first few classes were so hard, all I could think about was food, I could not pay attention and my focus was on the movement and sounds in my belly. 'Hungry Billy' as they called me, was very hungry right now. My teacher keeps looking at me; I'll bet she knows I am not doing any work. Hmmmm, what I would do right now for a piece of bread!

Thinking Moment?

Imagine - What would the world be like if people were all raised in a well-functioning family?

"Family is the most important thing in the world"

Princess Diana

Parental Duties Are Endless

Authors from all around the world have dedicated their time to the study of parenting and the role of the family and have written books fully focused upon parents and parenting. I have condensed this section on parenting, highlighting a few fundamental points, based on analysis from my interviews. Helping children to grow and flourish is not an easy job but it is worthwhile. A strong foundation is critical in the process of raising a child, no matter the family structure.

So, what is the role of the family? "It's through love and sheer hard work that we raise the next generation with the right values" according to Mr Cameron. He referred to parents as nation-builders. One of the people I interviewed stated that a parent's role was 'encouragement'. Others interviewed said the role of a parent is a great responsibility; they need to be caring, loving, understanding, provide unconditional love, provide guidance, and instil strong morals and values. One service leader described the role of the family as helping young people to develop socially and to grow up to be responsible, caring adults.

They went on to explain that we all need support, both children and parents. Families are under pressure; the media, via soap operas for example, provide representations of family life, which is not a true representation of today's family. Ultimately, parents have a responsibility for their children to ensure they reach their full potential. All human beings have basic needs; failure to meet these needs can have negative effects and leave voids that need filling. What are these needs?

- To know and feel that you are lovable and belong to someone – If love is not received, an individual may question their value. For some, if love is not present, it is sought after from anyone who is willing to offer it.

- A sense of being worthy – Individuals within society determine their values through different means. A footballer's value may be in the millions he makes, compared to another player. A homeless person may feel that they are valued when a person is willing to open up their home for them. A young person my feel a sense of worth, by the time given up by a volunteer each week to mentor them. Attention seeking can develop if a person does not feel worthwhile. "Look at me, look what I can do."

- A sense of being competent – Parents should support children to develop their confidence in their abilities and skills. If others do not believe in you or if an individual does not believe in themselves, the likelihood is that they will not try anything new, out of fear of failing. We all desire to feel that we are good at something.

The above can be linked to the theory of Maslow's Hierarchy of Need (a diagram may be found in resource section); all humans have basic needs that we desire to be met. These include our basic physiological needs, such as having food and shelter and the need for security, safety, love, belonging, self-esteem and finally, self-actualization. The first three stages are linked very closely to the needs identified at the start of this chapter.

A parent's duties are not limited to food, shelter and protection but parents are to support and guide children in their first developmental stages and provide the aforementioned love and attention and have confidence in their child's ability. This helps with shaping their knowledge and character and to prepare them for the world. Children learn to talk, walk, follow rules, read and write in the home, as well as at nursery. The home is the foundation of our learning and our first introduction to the world.

Food For Thought: The first 365 days of a child's life are spent learning and developing.

The Perfect Parent Does Not Exist?

If you are a parent, most likely you have made mistakes. No parent is perfect. The perfect parenting guide or handbook is not handed to a parent after giving birth and it is through sheer trial and error, learning from one's own upbringing and experiences, that a parent is able to raise a child. Children learn about the world from their environment and the people with whom they have regular contact. One of the main roles of a parent is to teach a child morals and values. Parents should not only teach them but more importantly, model what that they are teaching, as values are demonstrated in one's behaviour.

Children listen to what their parents say and many take their words as the gospel truth. Parents should be a young person's first role model, their guide through this world. When there is an absence of role models, at times young people go seeking for someone to look up to, to aspire to be like. It is becoming more common for young people to seek role models outside of the home. Let us stop making outside of the home, the place that young people look for role models on the streets. There is no perfect parent but there are key things that parents can desire to teach a child, to support with their development.

How Do I Parent, Where Can I learn, What Works And What Does Not?

Everyone will parent differently based upon their experience, upbringing, culture and knowledge. However, upon researching different parenting styles and also gaining some useful feedback from parents, there are some useful insights to share. Growing up, I wanted a mum that was like my friend because I had friends who had this but I am happy now older, that my mum was my mum and the person who laid down the rules and who I looked up to. We had clear boundaries in our house and I knew not to mess around. Well, not in front of my mum!

Parenting styles - Take a minute to think about your own upbringing, what type of style did your parents or parent use? This could have an influence on the way you parent your children or child.

There are four styles I would like to share, the first being 'Authoritarian Parents', who are typically controlling and strict and following rules are very important; children must listen and abide by what their parents tell them to do. Authoritarian parents are likely to say something like "Do this because I say so". "Do what I say, don't say what I do". I remember hearing these very words.

Then there are 'Authoritative Parents' who tend to be firm, supportive and motivate their children. These parents share an understanding relationship, explaining to their children why things need to be done, instead of just telling them and expecting them to do things.

At the opposite end to Authoritative Parenting, there are 'Permissive Parents', who are kind and warm, however, there are often limited rules in the home and children get to do what they want. Young people often say they want this type of parenting, when they have parents that are always 'on their backs', in their view. Finally, and sadly are the 'Uninvolved Parents', who demonstrate very little involvement in a child's development and life. A child will receive the basics of clothes on their back and food in their mouth and this is perceived as 'the job is done'.

So, which style is effective? The 'Authoritative Parenting' style has been shown to be the most effective because it balances rules alongside providing a loving environment, where a child can express themselves and where their views are valued and taken into consideration.

An Old African Proverb – It Takes A Village To Raise A Child.

Derrick Anderson, Former Lambeth Chief Executive, believes in the extended family, captured in this statement "I am not a nuclear person". His mother raised 16 children, 13 which were not her own and his grandmother also raised children that were not hers. In their family, they believed that if you have the resource and the capacity, you should help other families. In today's society, communities working together are more important and more needed than ever. As Pastor, Author and Speaker, TD Jakes said: "A star is not a star without its support cast"; it takes a community to raise a child and that includes you and me.

With parents having to re-enter the job market, this can reduce family interaction. Coming from a single parent family, I experienced and watched my mother work long hours to be able to provide for us. This is where support from the community can really help, as it is not just about watching your own children. Children in the same environments can influence each other, in a positive or negative way, so that community spirit is very well needed. Support in developing our children of this generation and generations to come, needs to be holistic.

#HelpOtherPeople'sChildrenNotJustYourOwn.

What You Sow, You Shall Reap.

Pastor, Author and Speaker, TD Jakes once said, "You can't withdraw more than you have deposited". I suppose parents hope that all that they have invested in their child will reap a good harvest in the future. A Proverb in the bible says, "Train a child in the way he should go and when he is old he will not turn from it" [Proverbs 22:6]. Parents have a role to train their children, to lead them, love them, support them and guide them. In my case, I was excluded from college, was involved in fights, smoked weed and was a 'little bad' whilst growing up.

However, I returned to my foundations, to the morals and values that my mum showed me by her actions, not just her words. There is hope because many people would not predict I would be where I am today. If you only judge a person by their behaviour, you may be missing a lot. What a parent invests in a child is what they will get out. If a strong foundation is laid for a child, when they are faced with decisions, a parent can only hope that they will draw on what they have learned over the years. A parent cannot control every action or decision that their child makes. From my interviews, this was evident.

Monkey See, Monkey Do.

An old saying, I often heard as a child was "Monkey see, monkey do". Can you remember trying on your parent's shoes or imitating your parents when you were younger? If you have children or have spent time with a child, you will always see similarities between a child and their parents. I am not referring to appearance but rather, characteristics. I often wonder why some children talk the way they do, until I meet their parents, then it all becomes clear. The passing down of morals, culture and behaviours happens unconsciously most times. What follows, is a story I remember reading, which highlights the passing down of practices unconsciously.

There was a woman who used to cut the backside off the end of the chicken. When she was asked why she did this, she replied "My mum use to do it". The question spurred her on to find out from her mum, the reason why. Her mother's response was similar "I used to see my mum do it". The woman asked her grandmother, who replied: "My mum used to do this because our cooker was very small and the backside of the chicken would stick out, stopping the oven door from closing". Actions and cultures are passed down from generation to generation, without us always knowing why we are doing some of the things that we do. Most habits are held, developed, nurtured and embedded from childhood; it is called conditioning. In many situations, dysfunctional adult behaviour can be traced back to a dysfunctional upbringing. Parents have a great involvement in the shaping of a child's behaviour and their outlook on the world.

If You Fail Me, I Hope There Is A Safety Net.

There is a wealth of information associating poor parenting and negative behaviour. Mariana Eizirik and David Simon Bergmann (2004) conducted a study on absent fathers in the home and the effects it has on adolescent development. Further, an article by Eliza Martinez on 'The Effects of Bad Parenting on Children' referred to research conducted at the Department of Education in England, stating that children whose parents made poor decisions regarding their upbringing, were more likely to have behaviour problems. Ineffective parenting affects a child's psychological, social and behavioural functioning. The consequences linked with poor parenting do not just affect an individual but also can become a problem to society.

It is evident that poor parenting exists; services outside the home now need to be the safety net for young people from broken or dysfunctional homes. If parents make mistakes - and some will - there needs to be additional support and services to be able to fill the gaps in development where possible. It is evident that some parents will not be able to lay a strong foundation, so what can be done?

If children need to be loved, given attention and to feel competent, what can you do to achieve the following?

How can you make a young person feel loved?

1.   Recognise changes in their behaviour or mood.

2.

3.

How can you give a young person attention?

1.   Take the time to talk and find out what interests them.

2.

3.

How can you make a young person feel competent?

1.   Recognise their skills or talents and praise them.

2.

3.

LET US TAKE THE POSITIVES THAT CAN COME FROM HARDSHIP.

Everything you have ever done has been in preparation for what you are about to do. No experience is wasted, as life is a process. Oprah Winfrey is a rich and successful business woman. Oprah had a hard childhood, without structure, direction or discipline, whilst she was living with her mother. Sadly, she was also raped. When she was able to break free, she went to live with her father, who could offer her structure, direction and discipline. Living with her dad was a great opportunity and turning point for Oprah Winfrey. Oprah has managed to achieve great success in her life, her hardship did not stop her and she has been able to use her experiences to help others across the world.

There are many other rags to riches stories, for instance, the film "The Pursuit of happiness" is one of my favourite films. It is based on a true story of Chris Gardner's struggles and hardship of being poor and living on the streets. Today, Chris Gardner is an Entrepreneur, Author and Philanthropist, living in his purpose. J.K. Rowling, the author of the Harry Potter series, was a struggling single parent. Howard Schultz, well known for being the CEO and chairman of Starbucks, was raised in the projects of Brooklyn and after his father lost his job, his family had little to no income. He was the first in his family to go to college and graduate. Poor beginnings do not always equal poor outcomes. Poor beginnings plus opportunity and support can equal a better future and a testimony to share with others in order to inspire. So instead of focusing on the problem, let us look at some practical tools that can be used by parents and professionals. If parents fail and we plan ahead, we can provide a safety net for the next generation.

#Ineverysituationthereisalwayshope.

Wrapping Up Time

The environment a child is raised within plays a huge part in their life. I will keep going back to this point as it is very important that the foundations are set right and if they are not, that there is support in place to fill the gaps. There is clear evidence linking poor parenting to negative outcomes and therefore, as professionals, we need to be ready to identify the gaps and provide effective intervention, advice or support services. Every child has the potential to grow up and reach their full potential; some people just need more support than others to get there.

Adversity should not always be seen as a bad thing, as it can make some individuals stronger. It can become their stepping stone to success. I believe that it would be beneficial if all parents had access to and learned about the basic knowledge of child development, through workshops and training. In the UK, to be able to drive, you have to pass a test but anyone can be a parent without practice or training. I personally believe there is more risk from poor parenting, than driving without a licence.

#2 Time To Ask Yourself, What Can I do? – How can you support parents in raising their children or child, being part of the "village that raises a child"?

Parenting Training.

"Each day of our lives we make deposits in the memory bank of our children"

Charles R Swindoll

Our experience with the world is likely to influence how we will raise our own child or children. At all stages of life, we need support. To become a teacher or a teaching assistant, you are required to go through some form of training because you are helping children to develop. So how do we expect a parent to parent without any form of training, guidance, experience or understanding?

This parenting training should not become available when there is a problem, just like parents prepare for the birth of a baby through antenatal classes, parents could be prepared for parenthood. A parent has the duties to raise a member of our society, without training or guidance; parents are left to explore via trial and error and we have seen some of the outcomes.

Parenting courses could offer some parents great tools for raising their child or children and I am aware that there are parenting courses available that are accessed by choice, or when problems arise. Not being a parent myself, listening to other parents' experiences and advice could offer many benefits, along with an experienced teacher, who could help offer useful tips. Every child is different but guidance and advice, I believe, is always useful. Children and young people are the next generation and if we can offer extra support to parents to help them on the journey in raising a child, what is the harm? One way to make learning programmes more widely available to all parents is to offer:

- Course before birth.

- Workshops during primary school age, delivered in job centres, community buildings or by schools as part of parent's evening.

- Workshops during teenage years delivered by secondary schools and colleges. This will aid with making the course more accessible and likely to reach more parents.

- Supporting parents to rebuild broken relationships with their children.

The benefits of schools delivering workshops, is that it can increase engagement between parents and schools but most importantly, the teacher will be aware of the needs of children, so courses can be tailor made to address current needs. Knowledge is key, through studying play work and doing a Masters in Youth and Community work, I learned a variety of techniques to use with young people, as well as knowledge. This was key to my journey of helping children and young people to reach their full potential and I believe parents too can benefit from a basic understanding of theories and techniques, learned and delivered in a fun and non-intrusive way.

Understanding The Power Of The Mind

"We are shaped by our thoughts; we become what we think. When the mind is pure, joy follows like a shadow that never leaves."

Buddha.

There was once this girl Emma, who loved to dance. Every day after school, she would go to the dance studio to watch dance practice. Emma would sit there quietly tapping her feet, recording every move to memory. For six months, every Monday, Wednesday and Friday, you could find Emma in the dance studio, never taking part but always there watching. Every night Emma would go home and practice the moves she had just seen at the dance class. She was actually very good at remembering the routines. July each year was the trials for the dance group at her school. Since starting at the school three years ago, not once had Emma attempted to put her name down for trials.

It was almost that time of year again, trial dates were finally out: Monday 9th at 2p.m. in the main hall. Jumping up and down with excitement were Emma's friends. Joyce, Emma's best friend, knew that Emma loved to dance. That morning whilst at school, Joyce looked at Emma with excitement in her eyes "Why don't you put your name down, you're always at practice, you may as well try out for the team" but Emma just played it off "I didn't want to dance, I prefer to watch". Joyce shrugged her shoulders and continued walking down the hallway. As she walked down the hall, Emma began to talk to God "God" Emma said, "All I have ever wanted to do is dance but I am so afraid, in my last school people used to laugh at me when I danced, even my family call me 'two left feet'. I know I can dance but I am too scared to dance in front of people." That night, whilst Emma was at home doing her normal routine of spending most of the night dancing, Emma's mum stood at the living room door watching her little girl dance. "Wow, Emma! I never knew you could dance, what happened to your two left feet." Turning around, shocked but excited at the same time, Emma said a little prayer "Thank you God!"

The smile on her mum's face, at seeing her little girl dancing and her words of encouragement that day, sparked something within Emma to want to dance more in public - something which she did not do before. I love this saying: "Sometimes you have to borrow someone else's belief in you before you start to believe in yourself." From my own experience, a confirmation from another about your ability, can kick start a move in you. The mind is a powerful tool, one that we may not learn how to master at school. One lesson to learn about the mind is whatever a person feeds the most in their life will grow, whether it is negative or positive. Emma did not believe in her ability to dance, she allowed the views of others to determine her abilities.

Thinking Moment?

Take Action: What is one daily practice that you can do to shape the minds of a young person?

" No one can produce great things who is not thoroughly sincere in dealing with himself "

James Russell Lowell.

Everything Starts Off In The Mind.

The most powerful computer in the world is the mind. A new born baby's mind is like an empty vessel, a plain canvas. Babies learn from their surroundings, being stimulated by sounds and bright colours. When a baby enters this world, it is collecting information from all around as he or she develops and grows. As we move through life, our experiences and knowledge are recorded in our mind's files. The mind is powerful. Author and Pastor, Joyce Meyer, stated that "Our minds may be like some computers that can have a lifetime of wrong information stored in them. It will take time to clean out all the old files and reprogram new information".

It is important that we lay the foundation right from the start, teaching young people about the abilities of others to have influence upon their mind. Teaching them to understand that each person can choose how they allow things to affect them or not. Author James Allen, in his book "As a man thinketh" likened a person's mind to a garden, which he said "May be intelligently cultivated or allowed to run wild but whether cultivated or neglected, it must, and will, bring forth. If no useful seeds are put into it, then an abundance of useless weeds-seeds will fall there in and will continue to produce their kind". James Allen, along with other authors I have come across, have offered some very useful statements about the mind, reflecting on these statements may be useful to bear in mind when supporting young people to reach their full potential:

- What a person thinks, so he or she will become.

- The mind will go where the thoughts follow.

- Negative minds cannot produce or attract positive things.

- An apple seed cannot be planted, with the hope of producing a tomato tree.

Mr Zig Ziglar once said that the biggest nation in the world is imagination; if the mind can conceive it, the body can achieve it. The thoughts of young people are very important in the process of supporting positive change. Daily, we are presented with information and pictures, as they filter through a person's mind, some information is kept, whilst others are discarded but these messages will influence us in some way, shape or form.

Educating young people about the power of their thoughts and how they can affect behaviour, is vital. Thoughts influence behaviour, right? So, if we could influence young people to think differently, surely this could change the output? A French mathematician, physicist, inventor and writer, Blaise Pascal, sums up the importance of thoughts, quite simply:

"Our achievements of today are but the sum total of our thoughts of yesterday. You are today where the thoughts of yesterday have brought you and you will be tomorrow where the thoughts of today take you."

How to change our thoughts: start by identifying your negative thinking patterns; what stories are you telling yourself? I am no good? Nothing good ever happens to me? Then ask yourself: are these stories or statements true? Do they serve you? If the answer is no, reframe your stories or statements, replacing them with positive ones. Every time your negative chatter wants to start, think about your new positive statements. After some time, the chatter will stop. This simple but very important exercise can have a great impact when practised; it can offer a sort of paradigm shift, which in turn will affect behaviour.

Remember, wrong beliefs and information in our life, which do not serve us have been imputed over the course of our life, so it will take time to change perceptions. We can support young people in the process of a paradigm shift, guiding them in the process of improving the way that they see themselves and how they see things around them, as it is said "thoughts become things".

Food For Thought: Did you know that how you perceive someone, is how you will treat them?

Tool – An Effective Tool For Supporting Young People: Coaching.

Coaching is an effective tool to learn from, when helping people to get from where they are to where they want to be. The role of the coach is to ask questions and allow the person to respond and find answers for themselves. Think back to the last time you supported a young person; did you give them advice or allow them to come up with their own answers for themselves? Often when supporting a young person, we use our representation and understanding of the world, based upon our experiences and knowledge, which at the time may be limited or different to their experiences.

In coaching, it is important not to project your representation of the world onto your clients. The lens which you see through may not be the best lens for another person. I have included in the resource section, an example of a 'clean conversation' with a client, where the coach does not give advice but asks questions based upon what the client is saying. Often, people sum up and evaluate what they perceive a person is thinking or saying, without really listening, especially when they know the person, or they have heard of a similar experience. How many times have you experienced this or done it yourself?

Author Stephen Covey would define this as similar to providing a prescription before even understanding the diagnosis. If you are in the profession of working with young people, I would strongly recommend developing basic coaching skills. I believe this will enhance our effectiveness when engaging with young people. Having passion to support young people is one thing but having the tools and practical and proven skills to move young people from one place to another in their life is vital for helping to bring about the change for the next generation.

How Do You Perceive The Young People You Work With?

Self-fulfilling Prophecy is extremely powerful. Henry Ford once said: "Whether you think you can, or you think you can't, you're right."

Mr. Ford was responsible for transforming the automobile from an invention of an unknown utility, into an innovation that profoundly shaped the 20th century and continues to affect our lives today. He was able to take a product and change it with a mind set of "I believe that anything is possible". What you think can or cannot be achieved with young people, will control the distance that you are willing to travel to support a young person. It is vital for us to support young people to see themselves in a better light, if the young people you encounter hold a negative self-image. Think about the difference it would make for that young person, if they held a positive self-image?

How we see our self is affected by people, events and situations that happen in our life. It is our duty to support young people to believe that they deserve success in life and are capable of achieving their desires. Most importantly, how a young person sees themselves is how others will see and treat them. A young person's self-esteem will affect how they approach personal goals and expectations for their future. I remember reading about a study highlighting the effects of how someone perceives you, is how they will teach you.

There were two groups of students, Group One with students who had a higher IQ than Group Two. For some reason, there was an error with the computer system and the groups where mixed up. This meant that the teachers were unaware of the group that they were teaching. The teacher who was expecting to teach the students with a higher IQ was teaching the children with a lower IQ and vice versa. The results were amazing; the students with low IQ increased their IQ scores and for the students with high IQ, there was a decrease. Why?

Perhaps how the teachers perceived the students, was how they taught them. If a person thinks a young person is an underachiever, how far will this person be willing to go for them? Many people will not go very far because they do not believe that they can achieve, so their perception is 'why bother?' The majority of people are likely to go the extra mile for someone that they believe in or can see is making an effect but how long would you support someone who did not seem to want to help themselves?

Tool - Counselling is a powerful tool for dealing with the past and also laying roads for the future.

Early 2014, I made the decision to train as a counsellor. Why? Because I wanted practical tools that I could use to help people to overcome barriers in their life, to let go of the past and walk into a positive future. I have a desire to see young people reach their full potential and I knew that I needed the tools in order to achieve this. Talking and listening is effective but I believe that having tested methods for helping people is powerful. Having received counselling myself, I know first-hand the difference it can make in a person's life.

However, counselling was not the path I took, instead choosing another course that I felt could provide what I was seeking, although this does not undermine the value I place upon counselling. This alternative came mid-2014, when I came across Tony Robbins, who is one of the best in the field of NLP (Neuro linguistic programming); every year, people pay hundreds of pounds to watch motivational speakers like

Tony Robins. After listening to hours upon hours of his conferences, I signed up to an NLP course. NLP is the study of excellence, according to Sue Knight author of 'NLP At work'. NLP finds the essence of that excellence – the difference that makes the difference. NLP helps people to find patterns that can be reproduced to achieve a desired result.

NLP is an excellent tool to use when working with young people. I had an amazing experience doing this course, an experience that I will not forget. By the end of 2014, I was a trained NLP practitioner and I now have great tools to use when working with young people and people in general. What often holds people back from achieving? There are many reasons but one that comes to mind is fear and past experiences. Now imagine you can use a basic tool to take a person through a process to overcome their fears and let go of their past, imagine the difference that would make? People pay hundreds of pounds to get counselling and what does a counsellor do? Listen and use tools to help an individual find answers that are already inside of them.

When looking at support which young people can benefit from, Toni Harriott from St Giles Trust SOS Project, said that effective support for young people would be "Challenging young people's behaviour and counselling was needed". She asserts that counselling would help young people to unearth issues that they are facing and help them to understand who they truly are. Counsellors have the ability to open a person up but also to close them back, as sometimes during a session a 'can of worms' may be opened. This is why having the correct tools are important, as young people come with many complex needs nowadays and when trying to help, there is a danger that you may open up this 'can of worms' that you do not have the skills to then deal with.

Toni Harriott has undergone counselling herself and stated, "If I didn't have it, I would not have achieved what I have so quickly, it helped me to understand other people and to accept them for who they are". Many schools have mentoring services within them, which have shown to be effective. Imagine if all schools in London had a qualified counsellor based in the school who all students had access to, imagine the difference this could make? If you have ever accessed counselling, you can most likely picture the benefits that counselling would have on a young person, if it were part of the school system for all to access.

The Mind Is Our Most Powerful Tool – Growing Mental Health Concerns.

The mind holds everything, our thoughts are gathered there, both negative and positive. More evident in our society than I can ever remember, are young people suffering emotionally and psychologically. How does a 13-year-old heal from a friend being murdered or even begin to deal with being witness to the murder? When I was younger, old people were dying - those who were sick - not my friends. Whilst researching about young people and mental health, I came across a website called "youngminds.org.uk" that stated some interesting information. Did you know?

- One in Four (26%) young people in the UK experience suicidal thoughts.

- ChildLine (UK) has revealed that it held 34,517 counselling sessions in 2013/14 with children who talked about suicide – a 116 percent increase since 2010/11.

- Among teenagers, rates of depression and anxiety have increased by 70% in the past 25 years, particularly since the mid 1980's.

- 55% of children who have been bullied later developed depression as adults.

- 18.9% of looked after children below the age of five (19.3% of boys and 17.4% of girls) showed signs of emotional or behavioural problems.

The exposure to social media, peer pressure and the increase in youth violence to name but a few, is having an effect on the younger generation. Young People are exposed to so much more than in my younger days, which is influencing the mind, which in turn, is affecting behaviour.

Wrapping Up Time.

There are a wide range of tools which can be used when working with young people, drawing on coaching, counselling and NLP techniques can aid with making the delivery of work with young people impactful, when used correctly. Passion to help young people is amazing but there needs to be more than passion and the ability to talk with young people. The mind is a powerful tool and it would be amazing if more youth workers, other professionals or those who regularly come into contact with young people, had counselling, coaching or NLP skills to draw upon. I believe that this will take the work that we do with young people to a different level.

Transformative work with all young people we meet, will help bring about a difference, we should not just inspire them but be able to support a young person to be able to bring about a positive and lasting change. Many of our barriers start in the mind, having the tools and understanding of how to support a person to change is beneficial. If you have not already, why not develop your skills in basic counselling, coaching or NLP? Learning to develop a young person's mind is priceless and so effective in bringing about a change, a long-lasting impact, personally and socially.

#3 Time To Ask Yourself, What Can I Do? –To help a young person Dream BIG?

A Tool To Try – Visualisation.

Visualisation is a tool very commonly used in sports. It is based upon a thought or thoughts that are repeated over and over again in the conscious mind, to create desired results. When repeating, an imprint will take place in the subconscious mind, attracting you to the people and events that match the images that are within. What is so good about the subconscious mind, is that it cannot tell the difference between what is real and what is visualised. A great illustration is an experiment by Dr. Blaslotto at the University of Chicago, related to the skills of throwing a basketball.

A group of students were tested throwing a basketball and their scores were recorded, before the students were split into three groups. The first group practised throwing the basketball, for a period of time each day, the second group had no practice and the third practised imagining themselves throwing the ball and scoring, making mental images in their minds. After a month, each group were tested again. The findings were very interesting. The group who practised every day improved by 25%, the 2nd group showed no improvements and the 3rd group who practised only in their minds, improved equally to the first group. There are many benefits to visualisation and it can be used in other areas such as relationships, finances and exams or picturing your self achieving. It really works. How can you teach young people to utilise visualisation? There are two parts for making visualisation work.

- **First** – An individual must clearly define what it is he or she wants (which may require some additional work with a young person if they do not know).

- **Second** – An individual must practice creating the desired outcome (in their mind) on a daily basis.

Take some time to try this it out with a young person and see what happens. For youth workers or parents, try having pictures on the wall that represent the desires and dreams of your young people around the home or in your centres. It has been said that 'seeing is believing' and it is often the small things done over a period of time that can produce big results.

The Journey Of Self-Discovery

"Be yourself; everyone else is already taken"

Oscar Wilde

There was this girl called Danielle, who was extremely popular and everyone wanted to be her friend at school. She was five feet five inches tall, brown-skinned in complexion, had all the latest clothes and all the boys wanted to date her. She lived with her mum and her three sisters. Danielle's family was well known, they were the family to never get on the wrong side of and most people feared them. Danielle was not a fighter but was a very peaceful person, was very smart and took her education seriously, despite her friends not sharing the same values.

If Danielle misbehaved in school, it was because she was talking too much with her friends, as she often did but she always made sure she made up for it by studying at home. When times were good in

Danielle's life, it was good but when it was bad, it was really bad. Despite receiving all the attention, Danielle had low self-esteem and she hid behind everything - the clothes, her popularity, having money and being smart.

No one would have ever known that Danielle was insecure, as people can tend to think that if someone is attractive, they have it all sorted and life is great. However, Danielle was far from happy, hiding behind her pain daily, crying at night, whilst smiling during the day. You see, Danielle had an image to uphold. What was Danielle's problem, you may be wondering? Well like many people in today's society, she was feeling empty. A void, not understood and as a result, she did just about anything to fill that void.

We are all striving for something, for some it's money, for others, possessions, success, power, attention, love, or the desire to feel valued, wanted and to feel complete. Danielle could be likened to a bath, with running water but with no plug, no matter what she did to feel better, nothing worked for many years. Until one day, she stumbled across a book "You won't feel the love, till you start loving yourself". These simple words changed her life. She learned from that point forward, some steps to increase her self-esteem and confidence but most importantly, how to love herself! She was now on a journey to discovering and learning more about life and with every day, she was feeling more freedom. Never judge a book by its cover as we do not always know what someone is going through; we all have a need and a story to tell.

Thinking Moment?

Food For Thought: How can you help a young person to start on their own journey of self-discovery?

#Bethemirrortoayoungperson.

Setting The Foundations Early On.

From primary school, children should learn the basic principles of loving themselves, accepting who they are and that there is nothing wrong with being different. The media presents to us every day how we are to look, act and the material objects to have in our homes - and many follow. With all the negativity in the world, what difference would it make to have positive influences, messages, pictures and workshops for children and young people? Understanding emotional wellbeing is valuable from a young age, as depression is extremely common in our society.

Typically, when working with adults with deep rooted issues, it can be linked back to their childhood. Therefore, it is important to educate children and young people about how to overcome issues, rather than allow time to pass without doing so. As it is said 'time is a great healer'. In all situations, there is a positive benefit. We may not be able to see it but it exists. Teaching children to look for the benefits or learning from a situation may be the process that they will later use in their teenage years, when facing situations.

Who Am I? The Journey Of Self-Discovery.

Issues within our society often stem from the way in which an individual sees themselves. WHO AM I? A question that we may all ask at some stage in our life! How many people do you know allow others to define who they are? Whilst with one group, an individual is one way and then amongst another, they are completely different. People often define themselves by their possessions, by others' expectations or by their achievements. I see this often amongst young people, generally not being true to who they are. Adolescence is a time where young people are more self-conscious about their changing identities, than at any other stage in life.

Self-identity is how a person defines him or herself, which informs a person's self-esteem. Based on this alone, if those working with young people support them with developing a higher vision of themselves daily, this will have a ripple effect upon other areas of their lives. A person's self perception is linked to their behaviour. According to Author and Pastor Joyce Meyer, many teenagers become involved in drugs, alcohol and sexual misconduct because of the threat of losing relationships, "Peer pressure". We all have a need to belong; however, some people are willing to do anything just to be accepted by others. It is much easier to do what everyone else is doing, than to stand out and be different.

Brian Tracy, Author of 'No Excuses - The Power of Self Discipline' once said "Your ultimate goal in life is to achieve your own happiness. No one else can do this for you" but we *can* teach young people habits and principles for discovering who they are, acknowledging that life is a journey. Think about all the thoughts that enter our mind on a daily basis; for some, this can be an overwhelming feeling. Daily we are bombarded with information about how to look, things to have and what we need via TV, magazines, radio, advertisements on billboards and even on the side of buses, social media and music videos; they all send out messages. A valuable tool when working with children and young people is to teach them about self-discovery and awareness. We are all on the journey of self-discovery.

Not Being Your Self.

Developing high self-esteem in young people should be on everyone's agenda. There is an epidemic of insecurity in our society, so developing self-esteem is especially important as it is about how a person sees themselves and how they will approach life. It was 10.00 a.m. on Tuesday 18th March 2014, when three boys came into the YPM youth club on a school day. My first question was "Why are you not at school?". Before anyone could respond, it was evident that one of the boys was drunk, who I will refer to as Ed. Ed was shouting and acting really silly; he was out of control.

Once my colleague and I were able to settle him down, we called his mum and took him home. At home that night, it dawned on me, why was he the only one of three drinking? I had not known Ed long but I could see from the first day I met him, that he was always trying to impress the other boys. There was something different about him; he was not like the others. I guess he was pretending to be something he was not because he wanted to fit in. I learned the next day that he got drunk because he was trying to show off to the other boys, pretending that he was 'a drinker'. Little did the other boys know, this was Ed's first encounter with alcohol. Sadly, I have never seen Ed since, as his mum moved him away. Over the last few months, she had noticed a change in his behaviour and associated it with his new set of friends.

A person's judgement of the world, their morals and values, etc, is connected to their self-esteem. Self-esteem is the evaluation of one self, based on one's view point of how things should be. Experiencing good situations can increase self-esteem but experiencing periods of negative situations can have the opposite effect. How well an individual is able to manage a situation will determine what an individual will take from a situation. Erik Erikson explained in his book 'Youth and Crisis', that identity is important throughout the cycle of life however during adolescence, young people go through more turmoil around identity, as young people go through changes in the body that can affect the way they see themselves.

The children development institute wrote an article titled "Helping your child to develop self-esteem" the following was suggested:

- Support children to develop hobbies and interests that give them pleasure, an activity for example, that they can do and develop their skills in.

- Allow children to deal with things for themselves without always jumping in.

- Encourage children to laugh.

- Support children with attempting new tasks and challenges.

- Help children to focus on their strengths and point out what they are good at, rather than focusing on their weakness.

Developing and identifying issues around self-esteem is important to address from a young age, to allow young people to be more aware of themselves and how they define who they are.

How Do People Define Themselves?

According Dr Andrew Dobson, self-identity is the understanding a person has of themselves and involves permanent self-assessments, such as personality attributes, knowledge of one's skills and abilities, one's occupation and hobbies and awareness of one's physical attributes. How do you define yourself? Do you base it on your past experiences, your present reality, how you see your future, your job, your skills or by what others may think about you? When I was younger, I based who I was on what I had or did not have and what others used to say about me.

Our identity is also coupled with our hopes, standards, goals, and fears. The danger of a person attaching their self-worth to a job, position in a friendship group, etc, is the consideration of what will happen if they lose their job or their position in a friendship. The likely outcome could be feelings of worthlessness and feeling like they have lost their identity. One day at work, a 7-year-old boy was upset because every Tuesday, his class went swimming. The issue was that he could not swim well and the other children always laughed at him. "You can't swim", they would say and he had to hear this every week.

I was trying to encourage him, "Keep swimming and you will get better, I am sure that there are other things that you are really good at?" Nothing I was saying was working, he continued to shout, "I'm rubbish at swimming and I'm no good at anything". After a while, he calmed down and went back to the session. It made me think 'wow, negative self-talk can start from a very young age'. I suppose this little boy defined himself by what others said about him and what he could and could not do and this is where it all starts

The Need To Belong

The great desire to feel needed or wanted can lead a person to do anything and everything to get approval. At times, young people get involved in situations that are negative and carry risk. However, that risk appears to be worthwhile for the purpose that it will fulfil. I remember this young girl, who I will refer to as Tia. Everyone used to call her ugly. She wanted attention and was willing to do anything to get it. She used to sleep with any boy who would sleep with her, to get attention. It made her feel needed, in her eyes, she did not have to be pretty to get attention.

Tia made a name for herself and not one that she was very proud of. As she got older and looked back at her teenage years, she learned that she would have benefited from learning about self-esteem and self-worth, which would have offered her long-term benefits, rather than receiving temporary gratification from sleeping around.

I was given a book called 'Approval Addiction', when I was at University, written by an Author called Joyce Meyers. I was a 'people pleaser' but did not know it until I read the book. I never said no, even when I should have. The need to please others was very important in my life, for many years. I wanted people to like me. I wanted to feel that I belonged. I understand how it feels to want to be a part of things and groups and to have low self-esteem. I can relate with others around the issue of low self-esteem and the wiliness to do anything to fit in. One of the benefits of my experience of low self-esteem, is being able to share with others, how I overcame it.

Replacing Voids

Gangs have a negative perception because of their activities, however what are the benefits of a group of people who hang together? Why do young people join them? Gangs offer young people a sense of security, a family to be a part of and for some, popularity and street credibility. To young people, there appears to be some positive benefits to being part of a gang, other than the negative activities. For me, always saying yes meant that people always needed my help, wanted me around - well that is what I believed at the time.

It is amazing to be able to help a young person leave a gang or to stop being promiscuous, however often that void is not replaced with anything. This leaves room for an individual to slip back into old ways, as a replacement is always needed when removing something. When smokers quit smoking, they have a replacement, whether patches or fake cigarettes or for some, they go cold turkey with a strong resolve.

As youth workers, teachers, parents or professionals, how can you make young people feel that they belong? I want you to think about actions you can take to help fill voids (voids being to be loved to feel valued and to feel competent with the young people that you work with.

1.   6.

2.   7.

3.   8.

4.   9.

5.   10.

"The best way to find yourself is to lose yourself in the service of others."

Mahatma Gandhi

What You See is Not Always What You Get?

Reflecting on my childhood, I was not really happy with who I was, I wanted to be someone else. I do not think I liked anything about me, apart from my body and that was mainly because boys used to always talk about it (the shape of it). I knew I wanted to make something of my life, I had big dreams, however I was not happy with whom I was and struggled for years to truly accept myself. The concepts of approval, self-worth and esteem were foreign to me. I would not dare tell a soul, how I was feeling about myself, no one would believe me anyway. To everyone else I appeared confident and happy with life but it was just a mask I wore for many years. It is very simple for an adult to say, 'just be yourself and stop following the crowd' but how does a person do that?

How do you deal with the feelings inside? How do you develop the resilience to be able to overcome situations?

Even adults find it hard to do this, let alone young people who have not yet experienced the world and themselves in relation to the world. Self-worth for many is dependent upon what an individual does, rather than based upon who they are. The playground is a big playing field and on the first day of school, everyone is trying to find their positions. You have the 'cool' kids, the 'normal' kids and then the 'smart' ones. Time and time again, I see children and young people trying so hard to fit in with the cool kids, doing just about anything that they can to earn their friendship and respect. It is disheartening to see that people would rather become something that they are not, in order to be accepted.

A Small Change Can Make A Big Difference

A study in the United States of America was conducted in a school in Long Beach, California. The study found that by changing the dress code, there was a decrease in crime, fights, and sexual offences, amongst other things. Why? Because changing the dress code affected student self-esteem. The way that they dressed and looked, gave them pride. Small changes like praising a child and giving a compliment, can make a difference. What small change can you make that could make a big difference to a young person's life? Below, make a list of 10 things which you can do today and for the next 30 days, put to action those changes, taking note of the difference.

1.   6.

2.   7.

3.   8.

4.   9.

5.   10.

Wrapping Up Time.

Not having a clear understanding of who they are, can lead to a person following others. Repeating an act can lead to a habit. It is evident that educating young people about self-identity, self-worth, values and self-esteem, can serve as a valuable tool. Understanding who we are is important and developing this process in young people from a young age, could reduce certain occurrences, such as teenage pregnancy, gang violence, underachievement, the need for approval and self-harming, to name but a few.

Addressing underlying issues, rather than just the fruits of situations, is very important, so that we are dealing with the causes and not simply the symptoms. A young person can work on their personal development through workshops, practical sessions and mentoring.

#4 Time To Ask Yourself, What Can I do? – If self-esteem is the foundation and resilience keeps an individual going, how can you help young people to develop these traits?

Self-esteem Development.

Self-esteem is at the foundation of a young person's life. Through our work with young people, helping them to develop self-esteem and self-worth is important in their journey of self-discovery but resilience is also needed on this journey, as there will be inevitable ups and downs. Below are some practical tools you can use and share with young people:

- Encourage young people to celebrate the small stuff (we should be our own biggest cheer leaders).

- Remind young people to not strive for perfection – no one is perfect.

- Support young people to focus on the things they can change.

- Convey the importance of young people surrounding themselves with supportive people.

- Teach young people to spend time learning about their identity, their likes, dislikes, strengths and weakness.

- Support young people to engage in activities that can help boost their self-esteem.

- Praise young people daily.

The development of self-resilience in children and young people.

"It may not be your fault for being down. But it is your fault for not getting up" Steve Davis. There will always be issues; there is no magic wand to wave away all of our problems. A child cannot control how their parents will parent them or the environment they are born into. What an individual *can* control is how a situation will define them (a victim or an overcomer). There are skills, knowledge and tools that we can use to help us along the way, to overcome the mountains, dark valleys; tools and activities to lead us into the sunshine.

#Resilience

Resilience is important because day in and day out, we are all faced with different situations. Whether these experiences strengthen an individual or cause them to fall will depend upon their resilience. Resilience is the ability to overcome the emotional, developmental, economic and environmental challenges in life. If a child has developed this tool, they will be better equipped to deal with situations and bounce back.

How To Start With Developing The 'Resilience' Trait.

This has been taken from the work of Edith Grotberg, a link to her work is provided at the end of this section. Resilience has a combination of features, according to Edith Grotberg, such as I HAVE, I CAN and I AM.

1. I HAVE refers to having people in your life whom you can trust, who set limits for you to keep you safe, people who help you when you need them (Key Theme: Parent and family role).

2. You are valuable, The I AM, refers to respecting yourself and others, knowing that things will be all right, seeing yourself as a person, who people can love and like (Key Theme: Development of self-worth and esteem).

3. You are competent, I CAN, refers to knowing that you can talk to others when things bother you, find ways to solve problems, can seek help when needed and can control yourself when you feel like engaging in negative activities (Key Theme: Development of skills and knowledge).

Resilience may appear to be easy to acquire, however studies have highlighted the lack of promotion of resilience development in the home. An effective tool when raising a child, is developing and teaching resilience and schools can also support in enhancing this trait. Below is a link to activities and resources for nurturing a range of resilience's.

http://www.bibalex.org/search4dev/files/283337/115519.pdf

32 Hours A Week Spent At School

"Education is the most powerful weapon, which you can use to change the world"

Nelson Mandela.

Let me introduce to you, Jodie Jones, a lovely young person, full of potential and hope for the future, in her own words:

Again, another late night for me, most nights I would be up until 3.00 a.m. My mind wandered yet again, to how I was going to get through my first class the next day, which was maths with Miss Mathew, at 8.50 a.m. I couldn't afford to fall asleep again in her class, as a matter of fact, in any teacher's class. With Miss Mathew as your teacher, you could not get away with anything. If there was an award for the strictest teacher in the world, it would go to her. Boy, she was mean.

With very little sleep, off I went to school the next day, extremely tired and barely able to keep my eyes open. Five minutes into the lesson, my eyes began to slowly close and I was unable to control them, it was like my eyes had a mind of their own. In my mind, I was having a fight with my eyes, 'stay open, stay open, please stay open'. I finally stopped fighting and yep, my eyes closed. What only felt like 1 minute was really 15 minutes of sleep, before I heard.

"Jodie! Miss Jodie Jones!" She shouted at the top of her voice,

"Don't let me have to call your name again; this is not your bedroom."

I was fast asleep but could quietly hear my name being called and the more I focused my attention on the call of my name, the louder it got. I was finally awake and I looked up to see Miss Mathew standing over me, with an angry face.

"Jodie!"

She said with a deep strong voice, "This is not your bedroom, now get up and get out of my class".

I jumped up, overtaking my tiredness at this point was the anger, I could feel rising through me. I shouted at the top of my voice, whilst making my way to the classroom door: "I know this is not my bedroom, do I look dumb?!". Slamming the door as hard as my hands could, my mind went back to last night. If only this silly woman knew what kept me up. The next stop for me, I did not have to be told, was my head of year's office. As I slowly dragged my feet, making my way to the office, the door was already open, it was like she knew I was coming; I walked in and sat down, normal routine.

 "Jodie, Jodie, here you are again, why don't you just go to bed early instead of staying up watching TV, going on social media or whatever you young people spend your time doing" waving her hands all over the place as she was talking. I didn't answer her, I just looked at the floor but that did not stop her, she went on and on and on. I ended up walking out of her office. If only she knew; 'why do teachers always tell you what is wrong with you, instead of asking you?' I wondered to myself, as I made my way down the corridor.

I could hear my head of year calling me but I just kept on going. It was almost lunch time by this point but I was still so tired, so I slipped into a class room to sleep. The sleep was great, a little too good because I missed my 3rd & 4th class but it was well worth it. As I opened my eyes I could see the time, I jumped up quickly and headed toward my last class of the day, with only a few seconds to spare before the bell. But guess who I bump into, on my way, Yep, that's right, my head of year, Mrs Lawson.

"Jodie Jones, get to my office now".

I stopped, turned around and headed to her office. For the second time today, I found myself in front of Mrs Lawson.

"Jodie, this school is a place for learning, not for sleeping and skipping classes. It is time to get your mother involved - you need to go to bed on time because it is affecting your learning. You're hardly awake in class and in the last two months, you have really fallen behind". Before she could say another word, I interrupted her,

"Call my mum, call her, she has more important things to worry about."

Being the runner that I am, never staying around longer enough to listen, I headed for the door once again; I had enough, I just wanted to get out of school, be anywhere apart from school and home.

 "Sit back down", she shouted in a loud voice but I kept going; I could feel the tears beginning to roll down my face. I ran out of the office, down the corridor, into the playground and out the front gates; I could not stop running, I needed to get out of there. I kept running until the tears were blurring my vision, so I had to stop.

As I slowly walked towards the corner at the top of the road, I just sat there, tears rolling down my face. I lowered my head in between my legs and closed my eyes. All I could hear in my head was shouting and screaming, I tried to block the noises out, I really did but I couldn't. It was like I was watching a movie in my head; there stood a girl, shaking and afraid to come out of her room but the noise was so loud, she was unable to sleep. As the girl moved slowly towards the door and opened it, ever so slowly, just enough to see for herself what was happening in the hallway. Her mum was lying on the floor, crying, while her partner – my dad - was on top of her, hitting her.

The movie playing in my head! The only thing was, it was not a movie but a replay of last night, a replay of most nights in my house. My dad would beat my mum every time he was drunk and that was almost every night. If only someone could help - but I was too ashamed to let anyone know. There were many opportunities to tell an adult but they were far too busy diagnosing my symptoms of tiredness, associating it to social media. In their eyes, social media is what keeps all young people up and away from their school work. If only someone asked me.

Thinking Moment?

Food For Thought: *"When you talk, you are only reaping what you know. But when you listen you may learn something new".*

Dalai Lama

#Whatsignsarebeingmissed.

8311,264 Hours of learning.

It is a privilege to educate the minds of young people. "Teachers should be reminded from time to time, how privileged they are to teach young people, they are privileged because not many people will have the opportunity to influence and shape a young person's mind in a way that will stay with them for the rest of their life" (Mr Devon Hanson, Principal of Evelyn Grace Academy). I had the privilege of interviewing many teachers, including Mr Hanson, a remarkable teacher, with over 30 years of experience working with young people. Mr Hanson has worked in over eight schools, all typically known to be challenging schools and has found great joy in his work. Teachers are in a great position to be able to shape the minds of children and young people, to be able to provide them with support and guidance that could change their life for the better. Outside of the home, school is a place where children and young people spend a large amount of time. On average, a child spends 32 hours a week in school and about 11 years in education, from the age of five to sixteen years. During these 11 years, a large amount of development and change takes place for a young person.

Children in England are privileged to have access to free education up to the age of 18 years. Schools offer a safe environment for young people to learn and develop for the future, with education being one of the foundations of a child's learning and understanding of the world. Teachers, unlike parents, are trained to do their jobs, to teach young people to develop, learn and understand. Schools have a distinct role to play. Mr. Mark Scott, Manager of Life Skills Centre, considers that schools are central to young people; "schools have a major role" he stated.

Derrick Anderson, Former Chief Executive of Lambeth council, stated that "School is what shapes you and the culture of the school will have a dominant effect on how you see the world when you leave." He went to a grammar school in Birmingham, where the school's philosophy was that they were preparing leaders for tomorrow's society and they had a sense that they were destined to do something, whatever that was in the world, for the future. Mr Anderson went on to achieve just that. Schools can provide young people with a sense of purpose; a young person should leave school, knowing that they can achieve anything that they put their minds to and be equipped with the tools and knowledge to do so.

One Size Fits The Majority But Not The Minority.

School plays a critical role in a young person's life but with everything, there is always room for improvement. The passing of GCSEs demonstrate one's ability to retain information and apply this knowledge to answering questions. However, an important question is how do you measure the application and full understanding of information obtained? For example, the alphabet can be recited as we remember it but when asked to recite it backwards or to start from the middle, some may struggle. For example, what comes after "I" and what came before, did you get it straight away or did you have to start from A? Or remember the alphabet rhyme?

Michael Young, pioneering social scientist, political activist and social innovator, argues that the schools in modern societies should provide young people with access to concepts that will move them beyond their experiences, in a way that would not be open to them from their families. Context-independent knowledge is normally the focus in schools. A wide range of knowledge is learned, which young people can apply to daily life. The problem is that young people do not often understand the links between what they learn and how to apply it in everyday life.

Ask a young person what is the purpose of wearing a uniform or even a tie and see what they say. I know many males in their thirties who do not know how to tie a tie because they never had to in school. I know how to, simply because of having to wear a tie whilst in school. One of the reasons for uniform is to enforce smart dress in school, which prepare us for the world of work. More evident than before are 6th form colleges having a smart dress code for their students. In my days at 6th form, you could wear what you wanted, yet if you dress the part, you will most likely feel like you are the part; dress like a million dollars and you may behave accordingly.

This resonates with and reinforces the message from the study undertaken at the school in Long Beach, California, as discussed in chapter four. Context-dependent knowledge delivered in schools, can aid with teaching young people how to apply their knowledge in the real world, from a young age. I have worked with many very smart young people who lack common sense and day to day skills. Teaching young people how to apply what they learn in school, is a useful tool, not just to be able to recall facts and figures. Not all children are academic, many will shine more doing practical tasks but school is mainly focused around exams and course work.

For example, I can do exams and course work but I am more of a practical learner and I can demonstrate my abilities better than I can perform in an exam.

What Did Those Interviewed Have To Say About School?

Mr Mark Scott, Manager of Life Skills Centre said, "School is the only place of normality for many young people, the only place that offers routine, rules and boundaries". School can be seen to a degree as a safety net, as development that has not taken place in the home can be learned in school. I believe school is the second greatest influence in a young person's life. Mr Craig Whittaker, MP stated "When parents can't parent, the school become the safety net". Miss Tracey Donnelley, parent and Manager of Children's Services at Young People Matter, considers the role of school as being there to provide education but felt that schools should not simply just do that.

Miss Donnelley suggested schools could, alongside education, offer 'life skills' workshops and help young people to deal with teenage emotions. Among those interviewed, it was evident that education is deemed a vital component, one of them concluded that "School is important and education is key". With more young people with complex needs today, I believe a school can no longer - or should no longer - focus solely on education. There are opportunities within the four walls of a school building, to offer young people much more and this opportunity should not be missed in the pursuit of trying to get to the top of the school league table.

Question: Why are young people failing, if schools prepare young people for the world of work?

Teachers Undertaking Social Worker Roles?

Mr Devon Hanson, Principal of Evelyn Grace Academy, stated that "Your schooling experience can make or break you". This was based on his experience as a child but also from what he has seen over his years of teaching. Mr Mark Scott, asserts "Teachers can no longer come into the class room just to teach, they have to almost play two roles, the teacher role and a social worker". In my experience, there is always a story behind a person's behaviour, especially young people who misbehave in school. Teachers have to play two roles, to teach but also to identify and observe the needs of their students.

There needs to be a balance between educational achievement and wellbeing. As one interviewee stated: "School should not just be one dimension, not just here to teach English but also should focus on student's issues". Mr Craig Whittaker, MP said that there is a need for guidance counselling in schools, not for post school advice but for support to deal with student issues. The wellbeing of a child can and will affect their education. Not all children come to school with an open mind, waiting to be filled. Some come to school with problems, without food in their bellies or even abused before leaving their home and often are still expected to get on at school and learn. Once we understand the core of these stories, we can be in a better position to help young people achieve.

The Other Side Of The Coin.

Teachers are trained to educate, not to solve problems...unless of course they are maths problems. Teachers study to teach a subject that they enjoy and most of the time, they may not want to come to school to do a social worker's job, as well as their own. For example, a teacher may feel like they are qualified to teach history but have little skills or knowledge related to helping a child to develop their self-esteem or to advise on steps about how to exit a gang. Praising a child is one thing but supporting a child to overcome abuse or to leave a gang is an altogether different task. This is where school could benefit from holistic working with outside providers, who are specialists in different areas. Is this not why we have organisations that specialise in these areas?

Schools are there to provide an education. However, the wellbeing of a child can have an effect on their education. Teachers may not be equipped to deal with or focus on wellbeing to the degree that some may desire or require; after all, some may see that as the role of the parents. A school's goal is to educate and achieve great exam results. Parents say school should do more and schools often say parents should do more. My view is that where there is a need, something needs to be done to meet it, other than blaming or pointing fingers.

Personal, Social, Health and Economic (PSHE) education aims to help children and young people deal with real life issues, preparing young people for adult life. Being such an important subject, the government wanted to look into making PSHE statutory which led to a review. According to the findings of Sir Alasdair Macdonald's report into PSHE, there were a number of concerns around making PSHE statutory, such as pressures on the curriculum, the role of governing bodies and the right of parental withdrawal from certain subjects and wider implications that could take place. It was said that "The depth and range of this learning experience should no longer be determined solely by individual schools and teachers".

One recommendation was for teachers to be able to deliver PSHE effectively, they would need training, knowledge and skills in a number of areas. Outside providers could be useful in providing the additional support to schools in some specialist areas, to aid with training of teachers and to support with the well-being of their students. Young people would benefit hugely from emotional intelligence workshops being delivered in schools, as part of an ongoing programme, rather than as a 'one off' event.

 # EmotionalIntelligenceispowerful

TEACHERS WHO MAKE A DIFFERENCE.

Can you remember a teacher that really made a difference in your life? Head Teacher, Mr Gary Philips, expressed that when he was at school, there was a teacher in year 9 or 10, who placed focus on individual students rather than on the whole group, which he believes made a difference to his achievements. Ms Ookolo was my best teacher at Lilian Baylis secondary school; she did not just want *me* to get a good grade in her class but always went the extra mile for her students. I am still in contact with her after many years. I can boldly say teachers, who do not just teach, make a big difference in young people's lives. Ms Ookolo instilled in me the belief that I can achieve and overcome difficult situations and I now pass on these same principles to the young people I work with. Who was that teacher who made a difference for you? How and why did they make a difference?

The Benefits Of Mentoring.

Mentors inside schools, who are not teachers, can offer great benefits. Mr Mark Scott, Manager of Life Skills Centre, stated that he is able to work with young people in a different way to most teachers, more on a social and spiritual level. He stated that it is important to show empathy and understanding for where young people are coming from. His job allows him to work with young people in a far more constructive manner. It is easier for him to do his job than a teacher he said, because his engagement with young people is based upon what is important to them and the issues in their life, which they need help to resolve.

Whereas a teacher has to teach, regardless of a young person's passion for the subject or what they are going through, the teacher has a whole group to teach, not one individual. There is greatness and freedom in allowing an individual to express themselves even though often people keep things inside and do not talk about issues or concerns. I believe it is very important to let things out, to the right people or person. All young people should have a mentor, not just those young people with an identified need.

Mentoring can take many forms, such as year 11 students mentoring year 7, to help with the transition from primary to secondary schools - and in all schools, not just some. There are outside organisations who are willing to come in to offer young people one on one support.

A Great Concern For Me In Education – Exclusion.

Its of interest to explore the question of what skills do teachers in Pupil Referral Units (PRU) have, that main stream schools can benefit from? Trying to work with young people in a different way instead of resorting to exclusion, I believe is needed in all schools and internal exclusions should be available across the board. There is something about having a similar set of young people all in one place, which is not always beneficial for their learning. My opinion is based upon the views and level of outcome attainment of young people I have met, who have attended PRUs. Persistent disruptive behaviour is the common reason for exclusion in school. Once excluded, the next place is often a Pupil Referral Unit (PRU). I strongly believe that it is vital to explore alternative ways for managing behaviour or engaging so called 'hard to reach' young people, rather than excluding a person. Author and motivational speaker, Les Brown said to "Align yourself with people who you can learn from, people who want more out of life and people who are stretching and searching and seeking some higher ground in life." It is very important and beneficial for young people to be in environments where they can learn and develop.

PRUs focus on a smaller group of young people than schools do, however I wonder if teachers in PRUs could also be used more in main stream schools; just a theory but they may have tools and experience for managing behaviour that could be beneficial in main stream school. When I was at school, you just knew which teachers not to 'play with', I would not dare miss a piece of homework or talk in their class and then there where teachers who may lack the ability of class room management. From my own personal experience as a student and from my experience with working with young people, young people know who they can try to misbehave with and those with whom they cannot. There are young people who find themselves in PRUs for many different reasons.

My Religious Studies teacher always used to say that I was going to fail her class because of my behaviour during her sessions. My behaviour was not extreme, a little bit of laughing and talking with my friends and if I got into trouble, I would talk back to the teacher. My teacher made a judgement of my ability based on my behaviour. I never failed her class, I achieved an A - my only A - I got for my GCSEs. Why was that? The point I want to raise here, is that a child's behaviour does not or should not determine their abilities, yes it can be a barrier but it does not determine the potential that lies within. However, the behaviour of a few, or even one, could affect the rest of the class - which is not beneficial for the learning of others. Having PRUs based in all schools, would allow for children to still learn within a school environment and to mix with a variety of young people. As we know our environment plays a big part in our learning and development.

Tools Schools Could Benefit From.

What are effective tools or activities that can be used in schools? External support, so teachers can focus on teaching, with external organisations coming into schools to provide a platform for exploring issues with young people in a different way.

Nicola Brookstein is the Director of Caboodle Arts Company Ltd. Her organisation uses performing and creative arts to explore educational, social and topical issues.

Nicola stated that: "Drama & the Creative Arts are wonderful tools for all young people, but they have an additional benefit to children and young people who do not excel academically. They provide an opportunity for those pupils to come into their own when looking at a subject in a more practical way. Children who don't excel in the class room can often be very creative. Our facilitators encourage young people to be unafraid to put forward their ideas. There are no right or wrong answers in drama like there are with Maths, drama is all about expressing your opinion or an idea and this can be very liberating!" Everyone has the ability to achieve; it sometimes takes the right support, opportunity and environment. Outside organisations can offer schools their specialist service, which in turn allows teachers to focus on what they are good at. I remember in YPM's early days, I used to go into schools to deliver sexual health sessions, with other organisations. For a whole day, schools would be involved in PSHE 'forced' sessions, delivered by outside organisations.

The issues with our young people are clearly there and many organisations are knocking at the doors of schools to be let in. I have worked in over 10 schools in Lambeth, however there are a few that I have never been able to access, as they do not offer an open-door policy for outside organisations.

Rapport Building With Young People Is Effective In Helping Them To Achieve.

What are the common things students often say about teachers? What I hear is "She's rude, man" "She talks to me like I am dumb". Now I am not saying all teachers are like this but with any human service provided, what is said to be important to get the most out of your client, student or parent, is building rapport. NLP has some really great exercises for this, which can be useful when working with people. I have worked in over 10 different schools over the last 9 years and I have found rapport building with children and young people to be very important. I often build relationships with young people quickly. One way is through making what is important to them, an interest to me. My main focus, when meeting someone for the first time, is to find out about them and allow them to get to know me before anything else. Mr Devon Hanson stated in his interview, that finding out how a young person is, is key.

#Firstthingsfirstlet'sgettoknoweachother.

Resilience Building, Thinking For Yourself.

"The function of education is to teach one to think intensively and to think critically. Intelligence plus character - that is the goal of true education." Martin Luther King, Jr. Supporting young people to build resilience is a life skill. Mr. Devon Hanson, Principal of Evelyn Grace Academy stated that resilience is key and "We need to teach our young people to think for themselves, to know what they feel is right or wrong".

In Evelyn Grace Academy, teachers instil the above process through teaching philosophy from year 7, supporting students in the development of critical thinking. He said that "we are constantly telling children 'do and don't' but we should be equipping them to think about why they should and shouldn't." Schools could benefit from equipping young people to think more critically and to have the tools to create the life they desire and to make the choices that they see as wrong or right from their point of view.

Wrapping Up Time.

Evidently, education is vital in a young person's life. Even if a school is outcome focused and prepares young people for work, the school has a role. Young people spend a lot of time in schools, so it is critical for schools to provide additional support. Schools should be seen as the haven for young people to come and learn but also to develop emotionally and socially. Teachers are role models, educators, social workers, mentors and they are the people who guide and support young people to reach their full potential. It first starts in the home, then school and then the wider community, like youth and community centres.

In order to provide a bright future for young people and to support them in achieving their full potential, exploring new ways of working with young people, is necessary. Some changes in the way things are done can bring about a huge difference for the next generation. With all changes, there will be financial implications, however, investing early in a young person's life will cost the economy less money in the long run.

#5 Time To Ask Yourself, What Can I Do? – To support the emotional wellbeing of children and young people?

There is no more evidence needed to prove that young people have more complex needs nowadays and that additional support is vital in the second place that children and young people spend a large amount of their time, school. An effective tool that teachers and professionals can use to have better communication with students alongside supporting their emotional wellbeing, is offered here: Communication & Rapport building - An effective way to be able to influence others is to have good communication and rapport building skills (Tips for quick rapport building).

- Use open body language – this helps a person to feel more relaxed.

- Make eye contact but not too much and not too little.

- Listen to what is being said and where needed, repeat using their words to show that you understand.

- Offer a compliment, avoid criticism and be polite.

- Smile!

- Find links between common experiences.

- Communicate in accordance with the person's system of preferences (This is discussed in chapter 10).

- Show empathy.

- Be non-judgemental.

- Be genuine and honest.

1. You may do the above already, however, it is important to be mindful of how we communicate with others when trying to build rapport and to seek ways to improve our communication skills.

2. One to one support for young people in schools – This will provide a platform for young people to have someone to be accountable to but to also have someone to express themselves to, taking the form of more mentoring in schools.

3. Finally, external organisations have specialist skills and involving them in 'wellbeing' or other programmes, could be an asset, as the use of external organisations means teachers can teach and external organisations can provide the necessary additional support. There are many organisations that are willing to lend a hand. Weekly programmes should be on a long-term basis and cover a wide range of topics, such as life skills, money management, youth violence and emotional wellbeing.

Every Little Helps

"Not he who has much is rich, but he who gives much."

Erich Fromm

Let me introduce you to Marcus Peter, a man with a heart for the community. Marcus lived on a local estate in South London. Marcus was 32 and loved to play football and he loved his job as an accountant in the city. In the eyes of the world, he was considered successful.

The laughter and chatter of young people could be heard, most evenings, coming from the stairwells of his block. The local young people would come to the stairwells, straight from school and stay there until 11 pm most nights. There was no local youth club; the only space was a little park and football pitch for young people to hang out.

There was a community centre on the estate but it hardly ever opened, it was mainly used for bingo and parties. Marcus's neighbours were always complaining about the young people hanging out in the block but Marcus didn't really mind because he could relate, as he spent most nights as a youth, in blocks too. One evening on his way back from football, he saw a few boys in the pit. He watched them playing as he slowly walked to the front door of his block. One of the boys kicked the ball, a little too hard and it went over the fence. "Yo Big man", one of the boys shouted, "I beg you get the ball, please". Marcus jogged towards the ball, which was beside a car; he picked it up and headed towards the pit. One of the boys came running towards him, stretching out his hand to collect the ball. "Respect for that big man". I guess Marcus was walking too slowly for his liking. Marcus continued to walk over towards the rest of the boys, introducing himself, "You want to play" one of the boys shouted, "Why not" said Marcus. He started playing football with the boys, they talked and caught 'bare jokes'; two hours passed before Marcus made his way back to his house. As Marcus walked from the pit to his front door, he was smiling. All night the boys were on his mind, in such a short space of time, he learned so much about the boys and each left a great impression upon him.

The day after his encounter with the young boys, Marcus went into the store room to get some footballs after his football practice. The club he played at always received donated footballs. He loaded up his car with 10 balls for the boys. As he arrived on the estate, he could see the boys outside the block. He parked his car and walked over to the boys with the big bag of balls. He was greeted with "Yo big man, Marcus, you good yeah" "Hey guys", Marcus said, "I am good thanks, I got something for you". Reaching into the bag, he pulled out a football and handed it to one of the boys and then another, until he handed out all ten balls. The boys stood there, smiling, Marcus could see in their eyes, they were surprised but grateful.

"Rare, thanks big man",

"Nuff respect for that".

"You boys are really talented; you should put it to good use. Don't waste your talents. Stay safe, I'm gonna head upstairs" said Marcus.

If joy of another person could be felt, everyone on the estate would have felt it that night. As Marcus headed up, you could hear chatter about the balls, they were not just any balls, they were top quality footballs. It did not even take five minutes and the boys were off in the pitch playing football. Marcus watched them from his kitchen window for about 20 minutes, before heading into the living room. Every day from that point, Marcus would stop and talk with the boys and after about two months, he started to take a few to Saturday's football practice at his football club. He entered four of the boys into a local club not far from their house and paid their fees for the year. Marcus was able to get three other friends interested in investing in these boys because he would not stop talking about them. Marcus was blessed to know people with money.

The boys were spending more time on the pitch, perfecting their skills and less time in the blocks, which made the residents happy. Marcus became like a big bother to them; he did not only play football but he also mentored them. He was providing them with opportunities and new ways of looking at life. Marcus, week in and week out worked with these boys, one month went by and then another and then another. Seven months went by and Marcus was still working with the boys and seeing a big difference; he was now well known on the estate and with their parents. Even Marcus's neighbours stopped complaining and were encouraging and thanking him.

One day he was telling his Manager at work about what he had been doing. His Manager, being well connected, explained to Marcus about funding that he could get to open up a football camp for the boys. He could see Marcus was very passionate. Marcus's Manager was chair of a youth charity. After two hours talking with his Manager, he was inspired and now committed to setting something up to help more young people on his estate. Marcus spent the majority of his free time for the next 3 months, researching and applying for funding. He set up an organisation with five other men who were passionate about youth. Their goal was for two of them to complete two funding forms per month, while the others worked on the programme of delivery and the business plan.

None of them had much experience in writing funding bids but they did not let that stop them. Form after form, they would receive rejection emails, yet they remained hopeful that one day very soon they would receive funding. The young people however grew more and more disheartened with every rejection letter. This great master plan was starting to feel just like a dream. They continued to apply for funding and did not give up; months went by and they were not securing any funding.

Then the long-awaited phone call came.

"Congratulations, you have been successful in securing £100,000 to deliver your programme." The hard work and wait was all worthwhile now.

The hardly every used community centre was finally going to be opened. The club opened five evenings a week, Tuesday to Saturday. Young people now had access to youth nights, homework support, football, boxing and cooking sessions. On average, 33 young people attended each evening. Over the next two years, they received small pots of money to do extra projects and to employ two part-time workers. Parents on the local estate were involved and volunteered their time. The future was looking bright. Everything was going well, until it started to become more difficult to apply for funding. The council were facing cuts to their budget and it was having a knock-on effect on local groups. Marcus was aware that three other groups nearby had closed and things were looking the same for them.

The project only had enough money to get them through another 6 months and if they could not secure more funding, they would have to close. Sadly, six months went by and the team was unable to secure enough funding to keep them going. Marcus and his team worked with over 200 children and youth each year and over their three years of operation, the team won awards for their work and young people's lives were changed. A once non-active community was now working together and making a difference. However, the closure of the club meant it was 'back to the blocks' but this time there were more young people with nowhere to go. Marcus and his guys continued to play football with the boys but it just wasn't the same.

Thinking Moment?

Food For Thought: If youth services did not exist,
would there be a difference in our society?

"We cannot always build the future for our youth, but we can build our youth for the future."

Franklin D Roosevelt

A Positive Youth Generation

Imagine for one moment how society would be with reductions in crime, gangs, teenage pregnancy, anti-social behaviour, young people in employment and young people without identity issues, completing school with five or more GCSEs. Young people supporting each other, instead of taking each other's life and young people reaching their full potential. Isn't it a great picture? To meet the needs of the next generation, children and young people need consistent and stable provisions, where positive and trusting relationships can be built and a difference made. There are many things you can do with young people for free but in order to support young people long term, stable (funded) programmes and functional spaces are required.

See A Need And Take Action.

Control the things that you can control and find solutions for overcoming and dealing with the things that you cannot. The voluntary sector, charities and local organisations provide huge benefits to children and young people, during the day, afterschool, in the evenings and during the school holidays. Most voluntary groups depend on grants from trusts, donations, foundations and the government, to be able to deliver services. There are small charities that depend solely on their local council for funding, unaware or unable to access other streams of income. The voluntary sector will be hit the hardest as a result of current and future cuts in funding. The extent of the damage long term, remains to be seen.

Funders and Trusts play a significant role in supporting community work; many groups would not exist if it were not for funding. You just have to open a newspaper, watch the news or look into a local estate to see that there is a need and with reductions, there is a possibility that those needs will grow. In the current climate, cuts to local Council budgets have resulted in Councils out-sourcing services to other local groups and this includes their buildings. Closures of youth provision across the UK have taken place. My own charity was hit with a 25% reduction in our funding, by one of our main funders. Children and young people need consistency in their life; if my charity had to close, there would be over 240 children and young people seeking alternative provision, per week. Sadly, due to 'postcode wars', it limits the services and areas that some young people can access; reducing accessibility to services. Who will fulfil the needs arising as a result of the cuts?

#Howimportantisyouthwork?

A Waiting Time Bomb.

In this current climate of funding cuts, for some charities and voluntary groups, survival is their only driver. Survival has meant changes to opening hours, increase to fees, lack of quality resources, more dependency on volunteers, limited free services and changes to client groups. Across the country, more than 50% of councils have cut their funding for children and young people's services. A survey conducted by the Guardian showed that a fifth of service providers interviewed, stated that the cuts have led to closure for their projects or transferring responsibilities. Cuts are reportedly a factor, contributing to an increase in youth violence.

My interview with a Commissioning Officer for the Council, highlighted that the cuts have had huge effects. In 2008-2011, he explained the council was able to support 88 groups with funding and today only 42-43 organisations. In the last three years, their budget has been cut by 40%. A warning from a charity head, stated that cuts in funding could lead to social unrest, similar to that in France, happening on the streets of England. Put simply, cuts in funding constitute a social time bomb waiting to go off. It is very important that youth services are adequately funded in order to support with helping children and young people to reach their full potential. Youth work is needed and always will be.

#WhereGreatValueIsPlacedGreatActionWillBeTakenToProtectIt.

The Closure Of Kids Company.

In 2015, 'Kids Company' - a high profile charity - was closed, with over 11 centres in London, Bristol and a programme in Liverpool. Kids Company started in 1996, in South London and provided emotional, practical and educational support to thousands of vulnerable inner-city children. The collapse of Kids Company sent shock waves throughout the media; it became a political issue, due to government investment of £4 Million, which was to be matched funded by a donor, which did not materialise. Mismanagement of funds and lack of funding were two of many reasons cited as leading to the closure of Kids Company.

The details of what did and did not happen is not my focus but the closure of Kids Company demonstrates on a large scale, the devastating effects that lack of funding and closure of services can have upon thousands of children, young people and their families. The government had to step in and provide support to these families. Unfortunately, the same support is not available for small grass root organisations, impacting young people's lives on a relatively smaller scale. What is the learning that can be taken from Kids Company? Governance of an organisation is critical; trustees need to be fully equipped and clear about their role. There is a call for tighter regulation for organisations in relation to money management, systems and sustainability.

I believe more still can be done to ensure children are not left by the wayside when funding comes to an end. I would end by saying that there is a call for more guidance and education for groups, helping with development and sustainability. Great work is taking place in our communities and often starting from a place of passion to help others. Helping others is admirable, however running an organisation requires more than just passion and groups often leave out the management side of things, focusing most of their time on the service delivery.

Common Mistakes Organisations Make When Applying For Funding?

Funding plays a major part in charity and community work and without it, many services would not exist to the degree that they do today. It is important to look for answers that can help organisations, so I spent some time with a few funders to see what they could do to help.

Lack Of Knowledge And Skills In Applying For Funding

According to Teresa Priest, from the Walcot Foundation, common factors that let down small organisations when applying for funding are "Governance, not having correct systems in place and not being in a good financial position to deliver the project". Another factor is projects costing more than the funding that a group is applying for and groups being unable to demonstrate where the additional funds will come from. One person I interviewed said that the fundamental problem when applying for funding "Is that groups don't check that they meet the criteria, so they have written a good bid but it doesn't fit into the funder's criteria and you get the impression that they have this good project and they are sending it around to various funders just hoping that it will fit and get funding". From my experience, I can say that this is very true, as I have done this countless of times, trying to disseminate as many funding forms as possible, in the hope that one out of the 20 would receive funding. If you have ever applied for funding, you will know how time consuming it can be.

What Can Funders Do To Help?

A practice which could be adopted by other funders, as a model of excellence, is site visits to projects that they potentially would like to fund. The Walcot Foundation, City Bridge Trust, St James's place and Four Acre Trust, are funders who seek to find out more about a project before offering funding. It really helps to give a better understanding and a feel of what happens on the ground. This is a great practice model which more funders could adopt.

Another useful tip funders can use, is seeking additional information before rejecting a form, when things do not add up but the project appears really interesting; what Walcot Foundation do is to seek additional information, to gain more clarity. Teresa, from the Walcot Foundation said that this could mean the difference between accepting and rejecting an application, as trustees are keen to know that the work they are funding will be delivered. Gaining that extra information, having first-hand experience of receiving additional support, I can say that it really does help in securing funding and also with completing future bids.

Funders have the opportunity to learn a lot when visiting community groups, whilst also being able to offer additional feedback to groups about their funding application. For example, from my own experience, funders liked the idea as conveyed in the bid but found that they gain a better understanding of the project on site, than from the bid. My learning from this feedback was to remind myself to write as if the person was from another planet and has no clue about the work that we do.

Feedback From Funders.

Applying for funding is extremely time consuming and most larger, well established organisations have bid writers. A helpful tool that funders could provide for organisations which are unsuccessful, is to offer additional feedback, as funders tend to provide very limited feedback on rejected applications. Receiving feedback from funders could help groups to improve their bids and increase their opportunities of being funded in the future, instead of them being left thinking that their project idea is no good, resulting in a rewrite or even abandoning the project. I am aware that this may be time consuming for funders, however if the common aim is to help communities and individuals, it would be worth investing the time. This way, funders will reach more groups who are doing amazing work but lack the ability to articulate their needs in writing.

Additional Support.

The Walcot Foundation provides additional support to groups around developing systems and creating infrastructures, which local groups have found to be very useful. There are not many funding bodies offering additional support, with only 20 percent of YPM funders visiting our projects or offering additional support. An excellent opportunity I was offered as a result of funding from a trust, was the privilege to work with five business mentors from the corporate world for 1 year, which made a huge difference for me both personally and also for the charity. 'The pilot lighters' is an organisation which links those from the corporate world with charities, to offer support for 1 year, free of charge. I had the privilege of accessing this service and it offered many benefits for my organisations, such as financial planning, thinking ahead and improving the quality of services we offer.

Capacity Building.

Teresa Priest, from the Walcot Foundation, expressed her concern that there is a danger of small to medium size groups missing out on funding as funds get tighter. Teresa has first-hand experience of the struggles some small groups face and the support needed. Small groups are often delivered by a person or group of people, who identify a need and have a passion to be part of making a difference. However, people do not often expect all of the paper work that is required when running an organisation. The passion is there to help but the knowledge of running a business is limited.

This is why capacity building is vital for small organisations, to aid with developing a strong infrastructure. Small to medium organisations could really benefit from a support forum, to help with capacity building and development. There are many groups that have the passion but not the expertise to deliver a long term programme. This was evident from my interviews and my experience working with other groups. I am often asked to help individuals to set up their own organisations because they see a need in their community and they want to make a difference.

Doing More With Less.

Cuts, cut, cuts, we are all facing cuts; organisations may feel forced to change their objectives to chase funding, becoming jack of all trades and masters of none and some charities may have to start operating like a business, due to funds and handouts swiftly decreasing. I remember when I first started my charity, funding was easy to acquire but now we have to come up with different ways of generating income, in order to survive. For some, the mission of the organisation becomes lost in the pursuit of trying to survive. It is really easy to lose focus because the funding is crucial in order to continue to offer services.

Over the years, I have experienced firsthand the effects of cuts in funding and having limited funds, not knowing where the next pot of money was going to come from. Prioritising available funds is a key focus in most local Councils, using funds for targeted services, rather than universal activities, where there is the greatest need. It is amazing to be able to support those who are not in employment, education or training (NEET), in gangs, or involved in criminal activities, however I agree with Mr. Mark Scott, Manager of Life Skills Centre who stated that from his experience, "Young people who are good, want to do bad things because, kids who are always in trouble often get offered more".

These young people are a part of a targeted service but are not the only ones who can benefit from opportunities and extra support. Think for a moment about a child who has struggled throughout life but managed to stay on the straight and narrow, pushing through to break the cycle of their past. They could benefit from a mentor or some extra activities that they have not been privileged to experience in their life too. They may not be displaying negative behavior but they too could have needs and could do with accessing new opportunities.

Support Is Available But Is It Really Support?

There is training available to offer support to groups with their development, as well as funding websites that have hundreds of funder's information, including their criteria listed. Searching for and researching about funding and policies can be time consuming, so having access to a wide range of information in one place is extremely beneficial. However, many of these services come at a price, which may not be accessible for an organisation with limited funding. They may not be in a position to invest in such a service, even if in the long term it will benefit the organisation greatly, with them having to instead choose to invest the money in the service they are providing.

Websites providing access to funder's information can range from £170 to £500 per year to be a member. For some organisations, £500 could hugely benefit the work that they do. Funders have money to distribute, thus an ideal service would be free of charge, giving everyone the same opportunities to access funds.

There Are Benefits Of Thinking In A New Way.

Things are quickly changing; I believe that organisations cannot depend solely upon donations and funding. From my experience, it is worthwhile having diverse streams of income or a business model of operation. Many organisations would benefit from the approach of being "social hearted, business minded". Income streams could be comprised of donations, funding, income from businesses, developing a chargeable service or product, or developing a campaign that would help to generate income, via a fundraising plan.

Solely depending upon funding from trusts is a thing of the past. YPM started off running a homework club for four years; after a contract came to an end, we turned our homework club into an afterschool club, changing it from a free service to a paid service. We now have four after school clubs across Lambeth and four holiday camps, which generate income for YPM to keep our other service running. YPM is able to remain social hearted through services users having access to our services that we deliver free of charge, for some of our charged services we offer a number of free spaces. YPM believes that all children should have access to new opportunities and experiences.

#Moneyshouldnotbethelimit.

Wrapping Up Time.

Where there is great need, focus will be placed, so let us not wait for an issue to happen. From my perspective, partnership working and sharing between community groups can help in the present climate. Investing in our youth will produce good outcomes in the long term, however continued cuts in funding will lead to young people having more idol time and we know what this could mean. There are amazing projects, offering amazing work, that need to be kept open, through accessing donations and additional funding. Improving ways of distributing funds could be one of many ways to achieve this.

#6 Time To Ask Yourself, What Can I Do? - How can you do more with less in the face of cuts and closures?

Think of five ways to increase income for a youth centre, which does not involve applying for funding?

1.

2.

3

4.

5.

It may be time consuming but additional processes in distributing funds could be effective in reaching groups that do not traditionally receive funding and are providing amazing work and making a difference. A few suggestions are:

- Video presentations for people to verbally demonstrate the need for their projects, social media is the direction things are moving, so this would be a useful forum when applying for funding.

- A change in criteria that ring fences funding, for example 15% of funding would go to small groups. I believe this will support with keeping many grass root groups open.

- Lastly, funders to provide more detailed feedback to groups when unsuccessful. A quick way of doing this is through using a tick box process which can identify the areas for improvement.

Business Model Of Work, With A Balance.

Perhaps it is beneficial for groups to explore different streams of income, as part of their business plan or strategic planning for the future. As it gets harder to generate income, new ways of doing so are required. There is a danger, whilst trying to survive, that visions can become lost, whilst providers become Jack of all trades and masters of none. A way to overcome this is planning ahead, putting measures in place beforehand. Easy funding and handouts are a thing of the past; there is a call for new ways of generating income and a successful way that I have found is having a commercial arm to the organisation.

Free Support Service

- Regular Workshops on different topics which focus on structures and governance.

- Templates on Council websites with information on how to set up a new organisation - Many groups set up and develop through trial and error.

- A-Z list of funders on all Council website, to help increase awareness and accessibility.

- Councils could support with running free workshops and provide resources on writing winning funding bids.

Increasing Survival For Grass Root Projects.

Access to funder's information should be more available to organisations for free; awareness of additional funding steams would increase opportunities for groups to apply for funding. I have included a list of funders in the resource section. How can local Councils help? Funder's information on Council websites can help with decreasing search time, whilst increasing opportunities to apply. If you do not know that there is funding available, how can you apply? These were a few suggestions that came out of my interviews with other organisations, youth workers and funders.

Questions To Ask yourself

- How important is funding to your organisation?

- Would you be able to still exist without funding?

- What can be done to help groups to increase their source of income?

The Benefits Of Youth Work

"We have a powerful potential in our youth, and we must have the courage to change old ideas and practices, so that we may direct their power toward good ends."

Mary McLeod Bethune

I would like to tell you about a young troubled soul, named Mickey. Mickey was a very popular boy in school; everyone wanted to be his friend. Mickey gained respect from his peers in school and on his estate because of his behaviour, as he was known for being one of the 'bad boys' on the estate. He was always getting into trouble but for some reason, it was a good thing to have this type of reputation amongst his peers. Mickey could not go a full term at school without being excluded and his mother was constantly at the school. One week he would be on half day time table, then excluded for three days and then back at school; the cycle went on and on.

Mickey attended a local youth club every day after school. He liked going there and the staff members were always happy to see him. He 'felt the love' there, unlike at school. Mickey's local youth club was like a family, they helped people out, would listen and hardly made judgments; in fact, the young people would say that staff members were like friends, even though they knew that they were not. There were boundaries in place; however, that did not stop the staff from forming effective, positive relationships. Mickey was a completely different person at youth club, compared to when he was at school. He showed respect to staff members and was always helpful but was still able to maintain his 'street cred'. Mickey was having issues at home with his parents; he felt that they did not really care about him.

At school, the teachers never listened to him and they spent their day shouting and complaining about his behaviour. Then at home, his parents were forever complaining. The only place he found peace was at his youth club, or on the roads. Behind all the antics, he was craving attention and the only way he knew how to gain attention was from negative means. Seeking attention from his peers, teachers and parents by getting into trouble, at least then someone noticed him. Mickey had a youth worker, as a matter of fact he had the same one for the last 6 years and his worker knew his family really well. Mickey had a lot of respect for his youth worker, James, who was always there to offer advice and support and was able to build good rapport quickly with service users.

James helped Mickey at the age of 16, through the transition of leaving a gang, using his own personal experience, to help him to get on the straight and narrow. Mickey left school without any GCSEs, however he had a positive attitude and the understanding that he could achieve anything that he put his mind to. James had a belief in Mickey that kept him going; at times when he wanted to give up, James was the turning point for Mickey.

Thinking Moment?

Food For Thought: Does going to a youth club have any benefits?

#Weallneedaplacetogooutsideofourhome.

Too Many Hours Not To Provide A Service

According to Jeffs and Smith, 2010, those who belong to groups are happier and healthier than those who do not. Neighbourhoods where there is community activity, tend to be safer and economically active. Where else can young people meet up all year round together, if not in a school or youth centre? Youth provision plays a vital role in a young person's life; there are too many hours available for young people between the end of school and midnight, between Friday afterschool and Monday morning and not to mention 12 weeks of school holidays, for young people to not have positive activities to engage in. If more reductions are made to youth services where will young people go?

Birthed Out Of A Need.

Today, there are many perceptions as to what exactly youth work is. A definition I like is, "Youth work is informal education for young people, aimed at empowering, educating, leading and supporting young people". Youth work provides young people with new opportunities and experiences to broaden their minds, to help them to reach their full potential. Youth work can be delivered using a number of methods, including mentoring, detached youth work, outreach work, in youth centres, training and via leadership programmes, for example. It is more than playing pool in a local community hall. From the words of Jeffs and Smith youth work is "A special set of processes which involves broad ways of thinking and acting, so that people can engage with what is going on".

A Change Is Desired.

My interviews evidenced the desire and passion of many, to make a difference in the lives of young people. It was amazing to hear all the different stories about how people got started working in this field. From living on the streets and facing hardship himself, Opy Onas set up his company, Proten International. Proten provides Business Start-Up and Coaching, working with disadvantaged young people, those in gangs, ex-offenders, those with low educational attainment or living in poverty. In 2007, I set up Young People Matter out of the desire to make a difference within my community, as a result of five youth murders in the space of a week, which moved my heart to action. The founder of BelEve UK, Marsha Powell, stated that "The death of my Mother motivated me to live my purpose and turn my dream into a reality'. Marsha Powell gave up her 15 year career in HR, to follow her dreams of setting up BelEve UK, a Social Enterprise that "educates supports, inspires and motivates young women to reach their full potential". The initial vision for BelEve UK came about in 2007, when one of her sister's school friends, a girl, was fatally stabbed. It became apparent to Marsha Powell, that the environment was changing and girls were also getting involved in risky behaviours; it was not just common amongst boys anymore. At the time Marsha saw little on offer for girls to engage in.

There are many CEOs I could mention, who are just average people making a real difference in their community, simply out of a passion to see a change. You have groups such as Self-Empowerment for Life foundation, Juvenis youth, Jenni Steels foundation, All Girls Rock, Young Mums Support Network, to name a few.

The Future Of Youth Work.

A Commissioning Officer stated that there is a future for youth work but currently it is difficult. He went on to say that youth work plays a really significant role within our communities because over the years, the scope and content of youth work has changed. Employment support for young people never used to be an essential part of youth work but now we are seeing more youth clubs and organisations responding to complex needs in young people. Youth workers to some degree, have to take on a role likened to that of social workers, helping and also referring young people. Young people come through the doors nowadays with diverse and complex needs.

Tim Brown, CEO of Raw Material said "The future of arts and creative services doesn't look great; it looks like everyone just wants to cut the funding in relation to art and young people. We need youth arts work; we need to promote a new type of youth work which offers a lot more to young people". A Youth worker, who did not want to be named, told me that they personally think that youth clubs will never die out because there is always going to be a problem "Unless you fix the toilet", which was a saying his granddad used to use, inferring that there is no point mopping up the water, you have to fix the problem. As long as young people have a need, youth work will be needed.

Jaja Soze, founder of PDC Music label and Indigo Youth, stated that if people keep relying on government grants, then youth clubs will close down but if we start using money to be self-sufficient and start building ourselves, this will aid with supporting and continuing good youth work, without fear of a service coming to an end. Youth work holds a fundamental role within our society and for this reason, youth work will always be needed.

Limitations Of Youth Work.

Derrick Anderson, former Chief Executive of Lambeth, offered many key points that left me inspired by his wealth of knowledge. When discussing youth work, he stated that "The problem with most youth services, is that they operate from a deficit model. In my experience, most good youth workers find creative ways of balancing out the deficit approach with their own approach to capacity building, even when they are not rewarded for doing so. The problem is the service, not the youth worker. Our policies always look at who is causing the problems and then reacts by putting resources into that area to try to fix the problem but only until figures go down. If we focus solely on the problems in our society amongst our youth, there is a danger of missing all the positive things that also happen."

A short-term fix for long term problems does not work. It is important to understand the difference between reacting and responding (or being proactive). The problems amongst our youth did not just arrive from nowhere, there were early warning signs and thus, it is extremely important to invest in early intervention programmes, rather than waiting for crises to happen. Prevention programmes need to be put in place to break cycles, reducing the opportunity of a repeat of what is currently happening and work needs to start as early as primary school.

Your Drive Inspires Others.

It is a privilege to work with young people and to be able to have an impact on their lives, no matter the size of the impact. A few words can make a significant difference, something as simple as 'I believe in you!' It is a humbling experience, when a young person comes back years later and says, "Thank you for making a difference in my life, if I had not met you, I don't know where I would be". It touches the heart and reinforces that you are making a difference and encourages you not to give up.

Trayvon Edwards, a young boy I have had the privilege to watch grow over the last 9 years, said during his interview, that I was one of his role models. Why? "Because you started from nothing, now you have a business because you worked hard for a goal" That really touched me because I never knew he viewed me in that manner. He always tells me I am 'cool but moany', so I did not really think that he looked at or paid attention to my own story.

We may not be aware of or always know the difference that we make in a person's life, simply by the things that we do. People are always watching. Starting Young People Matter at the age of 22 years has inspired many people to believe that they too can start a business and be successful. Karl- Lokko, an ex-gang member from south London Brixton, is doing amazing things, you only have to do an internet search on his name and you will be lead to many articles about his life and his transformation. Greatness is within us all, just waiting to be unlocked; there are people within our communities that can testify to that. We are all role models in some way or form, as someone is watching and learning from us.

The Difference Makers.

Being a youth worker myself, I am honored to work with the most amazing young people and am blessed to have the opportunity to watch them grow. All the youth workers I interviewed had a story to share about their experiences with young people. One of the people I interviewed said that his project has been "The best experience" of his life so far, in terms of opportunities for young people, which he enjoys witnessing. "Young people becoming leaders, you see team work, they become selfless, they encourage each other ".

Dan Charlish, Founder of Snow Camp, has worked with young people over the last 16 years, and said "I really enjoy working with young people, like you, I feel they are the future and they are the people that we need to be investing in. I think that there is a risk, if we don't invest in our young people and find them constructive and creative avenues to go down, that we will not be effectively resourcing the next generation that is taking things forward". As the next generation, young people need our support to reach their full potential.

Mr Devon Hanson, the Principal of Evelyn Grace Academy School in Lambeth said, "Young people today are more active and smarter than in my time and we need to tap into their energy and skills and channel them into positive things". At times, the problem does not necessarily lie solely with young people but also in how an individual views the current issues that young people are facing. There is a call for a new level of thinking, to be able to break cycles and aid with providing all young people with the opportunities to reach their full potential.

Many of the youth workers interviewed had experiences and stories to share about the difference that they have made in a young person's life; change is taking place and together we can make a great change for the next generation.

The Difference Youth Work Makes.

Louise McNestrie provided me with examples of her firsthand experience about the difference that service providers coming into schools can make, whilst sharing how good work can sometimes come to an end, due to funding. Below is Louise's personal story of change she has been able to make through her organisation "BeYou Training", the name of the student referred to in the example has been changed to maintain confidentiality. Sarah was a year 10 student referred to Louise McNestrie, as a last resort before permanent exclusion. Her anger and general behaviour caused many problems for her teachers and other staff. She would regularly punch walls and be aggressive towards her peers and staff. Over 6 weeks Louise worked with Sarah, building a good relationship with her. Finding common ground and interests, Louise was able to understand her motivations for her behaviour. Working with her on self-identity, friendship groups and setting her challenges, they were able to break down some of the issues and set targets.

The latter weeks were spent role playing situations and creating coping strategies that were less aggressive. Teacher and student mediation was carried out and a fresh start was allowed. Sarah worked hard to keep to her targets and to use her new strategies to curb the problematic behaviour. After the 6 week programme, Sarah rejoined all of her lessons and was allowed to join the school football team as a reward (something she really enjoyed). Using one of her positive motivations as an incentive, Sarah was able to focus on positive things, rather than the negative.

Since this intervention last year, Sarah has been kept in school and has not punched a wall in 9 months. Whilst she occasionally needs to use her 'time out card', she's settled in to her final year at school and is well on her way to sitting all of her GCSEs. Louise had a follow up session with her and Sarah only attended half of the session as she wanted to get to her English lesson to finish her work. Cutting the session short was a clear indication that she had progressed and wanted to take her education seriously. Louise has since been asked back to the school to work with another 3 groups of girls at risk of exclusion. However, funding for this project comes to an end in March and will no longer provide the much needed support for 'at risk' young people in that school. There are thousands of stories of great change taking place as a result of youth work, just speak to a youth worker and they are likely to be more than willing to share their experiences.

Perception Of Youth Work.

Youth Clubs on local estates are important but are undervalued and the perception held about youth clubs is what most people base the value of youth work upon. How do you perceive open access youth clubs for young people? If the perception is that youth clubs are a safe place for young people to access opportunities and learn, then it holds much more value than seeing it as a place to hang out and play pool with friends.

Colin Brent stated that "Open access youth centres must not be forgotten in the battle to define what youth work looks like today" According to Colin Brent, with the pressures to define the need for youth work, as more than just hanging out and playing pool, some youth provisions have changed because of the need to have quantifiable outcomes. A head of service interviewed for Colin Brent's report, stated that "Unfortunately the credibility of the 'open Access' session has diminished because too many practitioners think it is about staff and young people sitting around and 'chilling'". When hanging out with young people, I often have the best conversations and it provides me with the opportunity to get to know them more and as it is a two-way conversation, a young person also gets to know more about their workers.

When delivering workshops, there is often one main goal in mind, to provide young people with all the information needed to help them. Rarely does it start from a point of 'what do you think or know?'; asking if what they believe is true, the focus is upon giving information to young people, which can limit their creative thinking. A survey conducted by National Youth Agency, showed that universal youth work was vital in supporting young people; their study was based upon two key questions and they found that a large number of young people accessing universal services gain support for issues around depression, self-harming, suicidal thoughts and attempted suicide. Youth work offers young people access to information from someone to talk to and to learn from.

Colin Brent stated that: "For some young people, the youth centre is the only stable place in their chaotic lives. It provides a safe space, where they know they will not be judged. For some, it is a place to have fun, meet new people, a place outside the home to go, a place to flirt, for some a place to learn new skills. Some will pass through only occasionally; others will spend most of their free time there" Youth provisions provide much more than in previous years. You only have to spend a few hours in a youth club to witness the difference it can have on a young person.

New Opportunities.

Some charities are able to offer young people once in a life time experiences and an excellent example of this is "Snow Camp". They provide young people with the opportunity to go to the French Alps, to Ski for 7 days. Snow Camp takes hundreds of inner city kids skiing each year. Many young people have not had the opportunity to leave London, let alone, Ski. In our first year of operation, YPM afforded 55 young people the opportunity to go to Thorpe Park; about 40% of the young people had never been or did not know what it was. For me, Thorpe Park was a place I went to 3 or 4 times a year, when working as a youth worker in Kingston, whilst studying. If an individual wanted to look at youth work in its most basic form, it provides young people with space, in the evenings, at weekends and during school holidays; a space that offers support, new opportunities and guidance.

With Less To Do, What Will Become of Young People?

There is a danger of future reductions to services, leaving limited places or replacements for young people. Peers will lead peers more without youth clubs, indeed, peers will likely become their main advisors outside the home. There is that saying, "The blind leading the blind" and with reductions, I believe we will see more of the blind leading the blind. In fact, it is happening already. I once remember reading that you are the sum total of the five closest people you associate with most. Everyone needs a positive influence; some receive this from parents in the home and others from school teachers, youth workers or other family members.

When I was growing up, I did not really know about youth clubs, there were none on my estate, so hanging out 'on the roads' and 'in the block' was my youth club. You learned from the 'olders' and you mainly followed what other people were doing. The streets were just a stomping ground, as there was not anything better for me to do but I *did* know that I wanted a lot more for my life, than what I saw around me. However, there are a lot of young people who do not know what they want and the streets become the stomping ground and the place that many end up staying in.

The young people that I interviewed considered youth clubs as a place to go, outside of their homes, to learn new things, to hang out with their friends and to have fun. They spoke highly of their youth clubs and youth workers. There were improvements suggested, for example longer opening hours, opening on weekends and attending more offsite activities. Many youth clubs only stay open until 9 pm and most do not open at the weekend and at the weekend, young people have more time on their hands, than they do during weekdays!

Wrapping Up Time.

The seeds we sow in a young person's life today, will grow as time goes on. The purpose of youth work is to support young people to develop and overcome barriers, to achieve, to offer guidance, using a wide range of methods. Traditionally, youth provisions were perceived as a 'hanging out' place for young people to meet friends and play pool, however, there is more to youth provision today, which often goes unseen. Through decades of research, it has been highlighted that youth provisions offer a wide range of benefits and a safe place for young people. To gain insight, you only have to ask a young person about the difference a youth club has made to their life.

Youth services, just like schools, play a large part in a young person's life. Youth services are key in supporting and preventing young people from getting involved in crime, drug dealing or taking, gangs and teenage pregnancy, just to name a few. The big question is, if there were no youth services, what would communities be like?

Youth provisions fill gaps. There is a bright future for youth work; it just depends on what we do to bring that vision to light, which in the current climate, is very much about being able to keep hope alive. Youth centres can be like a second family, a place to go after school and during school holidays. It is win/win, a second home.

#7 Time To Ask Yourself, What Can I do? - To help improve community involvement and raise awareness of services on offer?

There are many benefits to Working together.

It is time to bring community spirit home. It requires money to deliver a service, however, it also needs people being willing to help, who have the skills and passion to make a difference. Take a minute to picture a community that works together, offering their time, skills and talents to support young people in their geographical area. What does that look like for you? How does it sound? What does that feel like? Money is needed, however with manpower and willingness to offer support and commitment to a project, a difference can be made.

If communities are investing in their community, this could aid with reducing costs, it can offer long-term support in dealing with issues but most importantly, it can provide individuals with a sense of belonging. Communities helping communities, more projects empowering members in the local community to be able to help others, to take a stand and to make a long-lasting change.

Think of 10 things to assist with and improve community spirit, in the community you live or work:

1.   6.

2.   7.

3.   8.

4.   9.

5.   10.

Mapping Of Services.

Across all boroughs, there should be a mapping of service providers that evidence all the services on offer for young people. This will aid with identifying what is on offer in each borough and where the gaps are. Many opportunities and services are available but many people are not aware of them. Awareness of services in your area could lead to joint working and best use of resources. For example, if group X opens on Monday and Tuesday nights and you open Monday and Wednesday and young people access both projects, what could be done to improve young people's access?

The opening days could be coordinated, providing access Monday to Thursday, instead of having young people decide upon which night to go to which club. I know there are many groups close to each other that do not work together, who work with the same young people and operate at the same times. Partnership working and general awareness of service is imperative.

Make a list of the organisations that are in your area:

1.

2.

3.

4.

5.

Visit or call each group and see how you may be able to work together or support each other. Let us work together to bring about a real community spirit.

#YoungPeopleMatter

#YoungPeopleMatter

Seeing The Apple In The Seed

Helping young people to unlock their potential.

"The first step toward success is taken when you refuse to be a captive of the environment in which you first find yourself."

Mark Caine

Let me start by saying, I do not want to focus solely on issues and problems, rather to search for solutions and tools to unlock young people's potential. A young person does not have to become a product of their environment. Imagine I was giving away £100, how many of you would want it? Now if I put it in mud would you still want it? If I put it in water, would you still want it? No matter what I do to the money, you would still want it, right? The money will never lose its value, regardless of what it may go through. The same goes for young people, a young person still has value, no matter what he or she goes through, achieves or does not achieve. The potential that lies within will always be there, just waiting to be released. I remember hearing a story told by Author and motivational speaker Les Brown, it went something like this.

There was a man who walked the same route every day to work. Along his way he would pass a house. On the porch was an old man in his chair with his dog beside him and on the other side was an elderly woman, in her rocking chair. Every day he would walk by and without fail, he would hear moaning coming from the dog. So, one day the man decided to stop and ask the old man why his dog was always moaning. The old man replied, "He is sitting on a nail", Surprised by his response, the man said, "So why doesn't he get off of it?"

The old man replied, "Because it hurts him but not enough for him to do anything about it". Situations at different points in our life can become overwhelming; at times appearing as though there is no way out. However, there is always a solution to every situation. If a person believes that there is a solution, then the mind will go to work, seeking out possibilities. Overcoming situations is not always an easy process but it is possible.

I like the saying I read in John Maxwell's book, where he refers to Mark Twain "The only person that likes change is a wet baby". Not many people like change but in order to grow and reach our full potential, change is required. Potential lies within us all, Jim Rohn said that we are to help others see themselves better than they currently see themselves. A person's belief in another's ability is very important. If an individual does not believe that they can do something and can help bring about change, the likelihood is that they will not try to. Our role is to help young people to see the greatness, to allow them to aspire to be more than their current situation.

Thinking Moment?

Food For Thought: Is it possible to hit a target that you cannot see?

#Greatnesslieswithinusall.

Greatness Is A Gift To Us All, Some Just Do Not Open It.

Inside us all, lays the potential to achieve; the same 24 hours is available to us all, the difference is what individuals choose to do with their time. Imagine a field with a farmer sowing seeds. The seeds represent young people. Each seed that is dropped on the ground has the potential to grow into a tree, a flower or a fruit, depending upon the seed sown. For the seeds to grow, there are a few key ingredients needed:

The Water: This represents support, guidance and daily advice given to a young person.

The Sun: The teaching of morals and values that a young person will need throughout life.

The Farmer: The disciplinary person, the farmer's role is like that of a parent; the farmer removes the weed and the dead leaves. The farmer monitors the growth of the plants to ensure that they grow to their full potential.

After some time, the tree starts to grow but the key ingredients are still needed, especially as it goes through the different seasons - Spring, Summer, Autumn and Winter. The wind blows and the tree needs to use its deep roots to hold itself up, the sun comes out and dries up the leaves and during this season, the tree needs more water but despite it being hot, the sun is helping with its growth. The rain comes and waters the plant and then the snow comes and freezes the ground and the tree needs to still be able to function during this time but just in a different way. With the right foundations developed, a child will be able to stand the test of time, no matter the season.

No matter the season, a strong tree will stand the test of time because of its foundations. Weeds grow unintentionally, however for some plants to grow, they require attention and young people need our attention. In order to achieve any goal in life, an individual needs to be intentional with their actions and thoughts. The same goes for helping young people. Young people will benefit greatly from intentional programmes or services that are based upon their needs and have been proven to work. The current climate surrounding our youth today, shows that more is needed. Youth violence is on the rise but by identifying the roots instead of focusing on the fruits, we will be able to achieve long lasting effects.

**Never give up on a young person, even when things are
not going right.**

Untouched Potential.

At the age of 22 years, I would have never started my charity, if it were not for Mr Marcus Dawes who saw something in me that I did not - the potential to make a difference in the lives of young people. Maybe YPM would not have been here today, if it were not for what he saw in me. For Marsha Powell, it was the belief and encouragement from her mother to just 'be herself', whilst working in the city. As a result of not giving up, she became the first black person in the administrative team, to make HR Business partner. Ask yourself this question: What do you see in the young people you encounter? Do you believe in them?

My skills, abilities, drive and knowledge was not enough to get me to where I am today. I truly believe that if it were not for the positive people around me and their belief in me, I would not be where I am today. There are many talented and skilled people in our society who lack belief in their ability, which sadly stops them from achieving their full potential. A significant key to a young person's growth is people seeing the seed within them that can grow to become anything. Every single person on this earth has skills and talents, whether they know it or not.

How a young person is perceived, will determine how he or she will be treated, in the wise words of Johann Wolfgang von Goethe: "If you treat an individual as he is, he will remain how he is. But if you treat him as if he were what he ought to be and could be, he will become what he ought to be and could be." Seeing the apple in a seed, is having the ability to believe a person can be more than what is currently presented to you. The next time you meet a young person, try to look past their behaviour and attitudes and think about the great potential that lies within. Believe in them until they start to believe in themselves. It will make a difference.

#Youngpeoplearediamondswithclaycoveringthem.

Your Environment Plays A Huge Role.

Author and motivational speaker, Les Brown said, "If you run around with 9 losers, pretty soon you'll be the 10th loser". When I was younger, I had many friends. As I entered into adulthood, I quickly learned that it was not about the quantity of people around you but the quality. We are influenced by the people that we spend most of our time with.

Toni Harriott, from the St Giles Trust Project, explained that, after coming out of prison, in order to achieve her future goals, she could not go back to the same environment expecting a different result, a change was needed. As Albert Einstein once said, "Insanity is doing the same thing over and over again and expecting different results". It is evident that our environment and the people with whom we associate, play a huge part in our life. I like the biblical scripture in Corinthians which says, "Do not be deceived, bad company ruins good morals." Peers will have an influence, whether positive or negative. Friends and environment were common facts that parents, teachers and youth workers suggested to me, were an influence upon young people. A person cannot always change where they live or the school they attend but can change who they allow to influence their life. Helping young people to develop self-awareness of what and who they are allowing into their life, is a great tool, as not everyone a person meets has their best interests at heart.

#Awarenessisalwaysthefirststep

You Cannot Unscramble Scrambled Eggs
(Problems Are Everywhere, We All Have Them).

All humans have a past and the past is something that cannot be changed, no matter how hard we try. For many, their past directs their future, which means that if a person has failed in the past, their belief could be that of a failure in the future, unwilling to try new things, out of the fear of failing. I love the words of Susan Jeffers, "Feel the fear and do it anyway". Pastor Joel Osteen says, "You are not defined by your past. You are prepared by your past." It is crucial to support young people to recognize that they are not their pasts and to encourage them to understand that their future can be anything that they desire with hard work, opportunities, self-belief and determination.

Hard times build character and resilience and with every situation there is something positive for the children to learn. Martin Luther

King, Jr sums it up nicely, "The ultimate measure of a man is not where he stands in moments of comfort and convenience but where he stands in times of challenge and controversy." Often people use their past as a comfort blanket to justify their actions. When young people are educated on how to use obstacles to help them to develop, they are able to process things in a different way.

Like a computer, when one understands all that it can do, one will be amazed. How a person chooses to let a situation affect them will be the difference maker. I remember hearing in a seminar, "We will all experience hurt in our life but how long we feel the pain, is a choice." Our minds are a powerful tool, however, like a computer we can have wrong data stored in them. I have met many people who have turned a challenging situation into an opportunity. Author John McDonnell once said, "Every problem introduces a person to himself". John Maxwell put it this way: "Problems are wakeup calls for creativity". I know a young woman who was raped and years on, she now wants to open her own charity to help young females. She did not allow her situation to keep her stuck; instead she used it as stepping stone to help others.

Food For Thought: Our perception of the problem, not the problem itself, usually determines our success or failures.

Seeing The Good In The Bad.

Author and Pastor, Joyce Meyers, in her book 'Approval Addiction' said that "There is no danger of developing eyestrain from looking on the bright side of things, so why not try it? Being negative only makes a difficult journey more difficult. You may be given a cactus but you don't have to sit on it". By educating young people to search for the positive in a situation, it empowers them to believe that they can overcome challenges. Learning to turn pain into gain and using negative situations as stepping stones, are vital for character development. I remember hearing a story that illustrated seeing the opportunities that lie within a problem, in a very interesting way.

There was a man, who owned a farm. The farm would flood every spring without fail but the farmer refused to sell the farm. As the years passed, the floods got worse, eventually killing all of his chickens. It got to the point where it was too late to sell the farm. The famer decided to go to his wife for advice. What do you think she told him? I told you to sell the farm years ago? No, she did not say that. She said if the farm is always full of water "Why don't you buy some ducks instead". His wife was able to see the opportunity in the problem.

Who Are You Feeding The Most?

Helping young people to change the way that they think, ultimately will have an effect on other areas of their life. There is a story I read in a Brian Tracy book, 'No Excuses - The Power of Self Discipline', which went something like this: There was an old man and on his shoulders were two wolves, one continually tempted the old man to do and say the wrong things and the other continually encouraged him to live to his very best. A listener asked the old man "which of these wolves has the greatest power over you? The old man replied, "The one I feed the most".

Food For Thought: How can you help a young person to feed the good wolves and decrease the negative beliefs in their life, aka the bad wolf?

Opportunities That Make A difference.

Opportunities can open doors for young people. For actor, Arnold Oceng, it was a childhood encounter with a parent in his school, who was an actor's agent, which led him into acting at the age of 6. Today, he has appeared in many TV shows and films and has recently completed his first role in a Hollywood movie called "Feel The Good Lie". They do say dreams can come true; a young person from South West London doing amazing things, turning a dream into a reality. He did not allow his humble beginnings to determine what he could become, or achieve in life, which many young people do. Today many individuals lower their expectations of what they can achieve in their life, based on their past or where they come from.

Arnold is now able to be a living testimony that great things can be achieved, no matter where you live and there are many more people like Arnold in our communities. Many young people just need an opportunity in order to make a difference. Another example is of a young man who always tells of his success being linked to a teacher who took the time out to teach him music, when other teachers gave up on him because of his behaviour. He was expelled from all classes apart from music, so he spent his school day in his music teacher's class learning music and making beats and today he is a famous British rapper.

Food For Thought: "A bend in the road is not the end of the road…. Unless you fail to make the turn" Helen Keller.

Your Past Can Be A Spring Board.

Instilling hope in young people allows them to not only dream but to dream big and to know that anything is possible. In the Book 'Three Feet from Gold' by Greg S. Reid and Sharon Lechter, stories are told of successful people using challenges to their advantage, evidencing the power of perseverance. I believe the more young people hear and see the struggles of the people that they look up to, that it will help them to believe that success is not just for a chosen few but for us all. We see Michael Jordon now but many do not know his story, which shows failure and a willingness to not give up. There are a number of tools and characteristics which can be used and developed in young people to help them on their journey, such as resilience, determination and faith, to name but a few.

Wrapping Up Time.

All young people have the potential to grow and achieve their dreams and there are a number of factors which can delay or stop this from happening. However, as people who come into contact with young people, we have the ability to make a difference. In every situation, there is always an opportunity for growth.

One of the many roles of a youth worker is to help young people to see the greatness that is within them. The more that we do this, along with other factors, I do believe a change in our youth will be evident. A person cannot change their past; young people have to work on the now and develop ways of moving forward and achieving their dreams. Developing a young person's self-belief and resilience is essential. There are many effective tools for working with young people; the final chapter of this book provides a list of principles and tools that have been suggested by those interviewed, to be effective and life changing.

#8 Time To Ask Yourself, What Can I do? - To develop a positive self-image within young people?

Helping Young People To Develop A Positive Self-image.

The ability to help young people to see themselves better than they currently do is amazing. Author and speaker, Zig Ziglar once said "it is impossible to consistently behave in a manner inconsistent with how we see ourselves. We can do very few things in a positive way if we feel negative about our self". Any one within our society, who holds a negative self- image, sadly probably was never shown how to think of themselves more highly.

Steps To Developing A Positive Self-image.

Step 1 - Changing negative self-talk by replacing it with positive self-talk:

How: First step is to get a young person or groups of young people to think of 15 qualities, Skills and talent they have. This is not always an easy task, so after five minutes, give the group or young person a sheet of paper which will contain a list of qualities, skills and talents that they can pick from, to add to their current list. You can also suggest to them a few qualities, talents or skills that you see in them, that they have not written down. Once the list is created, it can be used as a map of their qualities that they can look at every day, reminding what is great about them. (Please see 'resources section' for a list of qualities)

Step 2 - Replacing limiting beliefs using NLP techniques:

How: Youth workers would greatly benefit, both personally and professionally, from attending a Foundation NLP course, to develop some techniques to use with young people. Young people hold beliefs about themselves, as we all do but some beliefs held are not a true representation of who they are yet individuals often base their life-view and decisions upon them. Below is a Logical Technique to Eliminating Self-Limiting Beliefs and the link to a website with more information, may be found in the appendix of this book:

- Identify the self-limiting beliefs and write them down.

- Pick one self-limiting belief to work on at a time.

- Ask the question why you believe this.

- Gather any evidence that suggests this belief is false.

- Neutralize the self-limiting belief with positive visualization.

- Focus on your new belief about yourself every day, until it becomes a daily practice.

Step 3 - The development of positive habits - Teaching young people about discipline and its benefits.

How: Firstly, start by taking small steps, getting the young person to identify an area that they would like to improve. For example, to develop the habit of reading, a person can choose a book and set aside 20 minutes at the start of the day to read. Small steps in the right direction, increased each week, will help them to reach their desired goals.

Step 4 - Celebrate small victories - Encouraging young people to learn to celebrate small victories because it is the small victories that give us the momentum to keep going. Often, we do not take the time to reflect and celebrate the small achievements that we make along the way yet by doing so, it can be a reminder of how much we have achieved, which can help to keep us inspired.

Set Backs Are Come Backs
For Greatness

"My greatest challenge has been to change the mind-set of people. Mind-sets play strange tricks on us. We see things the way our minds have instructed our eyes to see."

Muhammad Yunus

There was once a man, let us call him Mark for now, who had a goal of becoming a millionaire, so Mark and his wife, Mary worked together towards their dreams. Sadly, on their journey, they were faced with the great depression. Mark lost his job and so did Mary, leaving them only one option which was to live off their life savings and eventually, they had to sell their car and home. In the midst of their circumstance, Mark still held on to his goal of becoming a millionaire, even though his future was looking very uncertain. Mary knew, in order to keep their dream alive, her husband would need to do something; Mark was very blessed to have a wife who believed in him and his dreams.

From that point on, together they spent most nights discussing ideas on how to stay positive and focused. Then it hit them, they came up with a great idea, to make and use pretend money to buy properties. This was turned into a game that they played most nights, it helped to achieve their aim of keeping positive, despite their current circumstances. From an idea to help to stay focused in the midst of the great depression, to a game that they enjoyed together and played with family and friends. After receiving amazing feedback about their game, Mark decided to approach companies to buy it. Mark was rejected yet despite the rejection, he knew in his heart that this was a great game.

The rejection did not stop him, he believed in his game so much that he paid for the game to be made and sold it in a department store himself. Later, a buyer came forward and distributed the board game, Internationally - and maybe even into your home. The board game is 'Monopoly', created by Charles Darrow. Just like Charles Darrow, young people too have dreams; some believe that it is possible, while others do not. Charles Darrow's wife supported him in keeping his dream alive and you too can support young people to turn their dream into a reality. To believe that anything is possible despite their current situation.

Thinking Moment?

Take Action: Today, make a commitment to support a young person to keep their dream alive. Who is that lucky person?

#Inspireyoungpeopletokeepgoing.

Failure Is Part Of Life.

"You will always pass failure on the way to success" the great words of Mickey Rooney. Picture a baby learning to walk, they try and then they fall but they try again, until eventually they are able to walk without falling. Now answer this question: How many weeks, months or years will it take before your give up on a baby learning to walk? Silly question, right? You believe that at some point, that baby will walk because it is coded in our minds that unless there are complications, all humans have the ability to walk.

What about young people? Why do so many people give up on them, when things do not appear to be going right? If our minds were encoded to see them as diamonds, rich individuals, full of potential and successful, I do not think that we would give up on them so easily. A car breaks down, we do not just leave it and say, 'that's it', we may get it fixed but there is first a belief that it can be fixed. I want to encode in our minds that every single young person in this world has the potential to be great, to be successful and to achieve their full potential. There are just often barriers and obstacles preventing this from happening.

There are endless stories I could tell of people who have failed their way to the top. Read the book 'The joy of failure' by Wayne Allyn Roots and you will find 101 stories of people who failed their way to success. In life, challenges, problems, obstacles and failures will come. The lens through which you see the world is what you will judge everything by. Every opportunity, no matter how big or small, has its challenges and every challenge has an opportunity; it is the law of the land. The law of human behaviour dictates that you will get what you expect. What do the young people you work with expect for their lives? Have you ever asked that question before?

Negative Influences Are Obstacles To Achievement.

The reason why young people are not achieving their full potential could be associated with several factors. Mr Mark Scott, Manager of Life Skills Centre, suggests that other young people (peers) and the media are major influences on young people and not always for the good. Mr Devon Hanson, Principal of Evelyn Grace Academy suggests that relationships, parents and how we conduct ourselves in public, all influence young people. "If we see children doing something wrong out in public, then we should correct them, not in an aggressive manner that may lead to an altercation but in a polite warm manner." Mr Craig Whittaker, MP, stated that family life needs to be the biggest influence in a young person's life. Their family life at home will determine or heavily influence the outcome of a child's life.

Children in care (such as foster care), for example, have low attainment levels in comparison to their peers who are not in care. Only 6% of children in care go on to study at University level and only 6% achieve good GCSEs (grades C and above) compared to 48% of their peers. Mr Craig Whittaker believes that in order to achieve better outcomes for young people, early intervention with families is needed.

Factors Linked To Lack of Achievement - Giving Up Too Quickly.

We live in a society, where people do not want to wait; a microwave society where quick fixes and taking the easiest way possible is the norm. A teacher I interviewed explained that, whilst at school, things come easily to young people. However, once they leave school, many find it hard because they were dependent on the school system to do things for them, rather than developing the skills to be independent. This highlights the importance of developing resiliences in young people. If a situation presents a challenge, some young people are likely to give up than to push through.

From reception age, up until the age of 16 years, education is not really a choice; now after completing tertiary education at 16 years, young people have to do one of the following until they reach 18 years: apprentices, full–time education or volunteering. Once a young person enters into education each year, students move up whether or not they are performing to the level set for that age group. After this point, the hard work begins, you no longer just move up a level, or move up a class at school, you have to apply for colleges, make the grades or find a job, young people start to become more independent or should I say, 'should be' at this point.

Food For Thought: Developing resilience and perseverance in young people is key to their personal development and growth.

Foundational Gaps.

Our lives are governed by our values. Ask a young person what their values are and pay attention to what they say. Many do not actually know. The more I open up the newspaper or see on social media that another life has been taken, the more I question the value placed on life by a few young people. Marsha Powell stated that "Young people have lost their morals that they have been taught by their families and others. Many young people's morals have been diluted down by the things that they watch, play and hear in their environments". The media depicts negative images, it somehow paralyses us to believe there is no hope, we rarely hear of young people becoming entrepreneurs, young people achieving amazing results at school or developing products or apps. What hope does a young person really have in their minds, if all they see is negativity?

Many young people are out there just trying to survive, with a mentally of 'it is you or me'. There is so much negatively around us and for some young people, there is a need to re-learn what 'caring for others' really means and entails. It is a huge concern of mine, that young people are being killed by other young people. It is becoming too common and it must be stopped; a whole book can be dedicated to youth violence. However, addressing the root is what will bring about an effective change, to treat the causes and not focus on the symptoms only.

Time For Action: Think of five ways to support young people to develop and identify their values.

1.

2.

3.

4.

5.

When we begin to think of ways of dealing with things, we can start to tackle the problem, e.g.: think of 50 ways to overcome youth violence. This allows the mind to go to work and to creatively think of solutions to current problems.

Awareness Of Opportunity.

There are many opportunities on offer for young people, however there are many young people who do not know about them. Rachel Beckles, former employee of '4children' and Dan Charlish, Founder of Snow Camp suggest that there need to be more opportunities that young people want and need to engage with. Opportunities open the doors and can also open the minds of young people. Take a young person out of their everyday surroundings and just observe the difference. You can be greatly influenced by your environment. Having the opportunity to take young people to the French Alps was amazing - they still talk about it today, it had such a huge impact on them. This was a once in a life time experience for many, including me.

The Missing Piece To The Puzzle.

Professionals, parents and young people were asked the question 'What are young people missing?' The list was endless; answers varied from behavioural problems, lack of respect, low self-esteem, lack of confidence and even mental health issues. The main point suggested was that young people are missing guidance. Some of the comments made, are cited below. One professional interviewed for this book believes that young people are missing encouragement and support, conveying: "I think a lot of our young people are left to their own devices", young people are living up to media perception and turning to the roads and TV for guidance.

Toni Harriott, from St Giles Trust Project, believes that young people are missing role models and mentors, to provide them with positive attitudes and better opportunities. Toni Harriott went on to say, "We need to inspire young people to want to achieve, which I think that they all can" It is very easy to say that young people just want to 'doss around', be lazy and smoke weed (in some cases), but that is just a negative attitude to have towards the next generation, who will be running the world in a few decades". No matter who we are or what we do, or how old we get, we all need guidance and advice at different points in our lives.

Wrapping Up Time.

There are many different factors that can affect a young person's ability to reach their full potential. First things first, we need to identify the effects and then come up with solutions to address each thing that has been identified. If we can identify why they are failing, it is easier to look for the solutions to help them to achieve. With time being an important factor, people often do the best that they can, with what they have at that time. A young person with a limiting belief that they are not good enough is doing the best that they can with that mind-set, depending upon their own knowledge and understanding.

The mind will not allow them to push for greatness, if they do not believe that they deserve it. With the right support and guidance, young people can be directed onto the right path for them. There are many side roads that we may embark upon whilst working towards our goals but the great things is, all side roads lead back to the main road. We are not our past, but our past shapes who we are today, therefore, problems can make us stronger and wiser. Despite having a destructive past, complicated family or a somewhat negative outlook on life, there is hope for young people. We just have to be willing to find the solutions; when one thing does not work, we have to try a new approach.

There are people who have experienced situations one cannot even imagine but have overcome. Some young people are failing but small and effective tools can be used to help them on their path to reaching their full potential. A safety net is always vital when working with young people; when things do not go to plan, a back-up plan is needed. I have mentioned a few tools that are effective when working with young people and I hope that they will help you, as you help others. There is not one quick fix solution, it is going to take time and effort to address current issues.

#9 Time To Ask Yourself, What Can I do? – to help young people make small but significant steps in the right direction (Life's Game Plan)?

Small steps in the right direction, over a period of time, will make a difference. **#CompoundEffect**

Darren Hardy's Game Plan For Life.

We are all role models in one way or another, singers, actors, entertainers, neighbours are role models, even when they have not signed up to do so. We have the power to influence those around us, in a negative or positive way and often without knowing. An Action Guidance Plan is a document that I believe will be beneficial to all young people; the guide looks at:

- Where they are (current state in life).

- What the gaps are.

- Plans for their future.

There needs to be questions asked along the way, whilst completing this document. For example, questions such as

- Why?

- What?

- How?

- By when?

To help encourage an individual's thinking, e.g.: why do you want X? When you have X, how will it make you feel? Anyone can write goals upon a piece of paper, however implementing your goals is the next step. When working on goal setting with young people, do not just get them to write it down goals but to also think about how they will feel once they achieve their goals. A tool to encourage daily, is to help young people to visualize their goals.

The Action Guidance Plan can be used as a referral point for a young person to be referred onto other programmes or services for additional support. It is a document that a young person can reflect upon and review throughout their life, adding to it as they get older, exploring the following:

- Identify what a young person wants and why they want it.

- Find the barriers that can or are stopping them from achieving what they want.

- Provide steps to achieving their goals - Support needed - Time frames - and how to achieve desired goals (game plan)

- Time to Act – Identifying and focusing on daily, acts that will turn into habits overtime. Developing the disciplines that are needed to support achievement of desired goals.

- Set small goals which can be achieved within 1 week, 1 month, 6 months. Take each area one at a time and aim to be disciplined, until it becomes a habit before moving onto the next goal, repeating the same thing, until habits are formed in all goal areas.

- After some time, review the plan to examine progress and make adjustments where possible. It is a great feeling to look back at goals set and to see distance travelled.

Food For Thought: *"Every well-built house started with a definite plan, in the form of a blue print"*

Napoleon Hill

Change Makers

Tools For Working With Young People

"Some men see things as they are and say, why? I dream of things that never were and say Why not?"

George Bernard Shaw

Life is a journey not a destination, the only thing that is guaranteed in life is death. Spring, Summer, Autumn and Winter are the different seasons we experience every year without fail. Just like the seasons of weather, there are seasons that one will go through in life. There will be seasons of greatness, seasons of pain, seasons of sadness and seasons of joy. That is life, things will not always go to plan but how individuals perceive a situation will determine their attitude towards how they will respond or react.

Discovering tools, activities and skills was the purpose of this book, with the aim of helping children and young people to reach their full potential. The previous chapters have presented information and the experiences of others, I pray that this book has served you in some way. It is in taking action that we can bring about a change, the words that keep me going in hard or uncertain times, are that:

"It's never too late to be what you might have been." – George Elliot.

It is never too late to help a young person, it is never too late to change our communities; it will only be too late if we never try. I have put together 10 practical ways of helping young people, based on advice from parents, teachers, youth workers, MPs, young people and community members. These are tools that people have found to be powerful, useful and meaningful for helping children and young people.

The Big Question: What works? What is the difference that will make the difference in the life of a young person?

#Relationship

Tool 1 - Relationship Is The Foundation To Helping A Young Person.

The number one top tool to develop is the ability to build positive and effective relationships. At the heart of helping and connecting with others is trust. Is this a tool? Yes, it is. Any good relationship is built on a foundation of trust, in order to help someone, you have to know their needs, likes, wants, desires and hurts. You can give a homeless person money without knowing them but just because you have given them money does not mean you have helped them.

The help I am referring to is long term impact, sowing of seeds that may not flourish in the present but will in due course. Relationship is key in the quest to support children and young people to reach their full potential. How can you help me if you do not know me? A very good question to ask.

An individual must connect in order to affect, if there is no connect, there is no effect. The first steps in trying to help a young person, is to build rapport as effective youth work involves making connections. Below is a website that conveys information on building rapport that you may find useful. https://www.mindtools.com/pages/article/buildingrapport.htm (Rapport Building).

John Maxwell once said, "People open up to people they can trust". From my experience, building relationships before trying to help has been very effective in the process. I have developed more effective and long-lasting relationships, achieving positive outcomes, when I first try to understand who an individual is and allow time for trust to be built. A young person is more than their problem. Get to know them and not just their problem. The key to human relationship is making others feel important; as humans, we desire connection with others. If you want to get a different result, try a different approach.

#Communication

Tool 2 Effective Communication Opens Hearts And Doors.

We all have the ability to communicate; we do it every day but possessing the ability to communicate successfully is another thing. Think back to a time when you have felt someone had communicated really poorly? Maybe the person did one of the following:

1. Jumped in and made an assumption before even finding out the full story.

2. The person was very forward and loud.

3. The person was a mind reader, telling you how you must feel and what you should and should not do.

Ever experienced any of the above? I feel it is likely. Everything we do involves communication and effective communication is the second top tool to develop. What is said is only part of communication, how it is said is critical; the pitch, the rate, volume, facial expression. People pay to learn how to communicate effectively. Content is tied to delivery; if the delivery is bad, it does not matter how powerful the content is, it can get lost. Communication is part of our everyday lives, we communicate with others not just by the words that we say but through pictures, text, facial expression and even our clothes.

Words are powerful, take Barack Obama's winning election speech; it touched the hearts of the people. Why? Because his message had a purpose and that was to engage, inspire, create an enticing vision for the future, to move people to action and he did just that. Adolf Hitler, with the use of words, was able to lead people to kill. There is power in the words we use, to build people up or bring them down. Proverbs 18:21 says "Death and life are in the power of the tongue, and those who love its use will eat its fruit." When communicating with young people it is important to be mindful of the words that are used, words should be used to uplift, inspire, and move individuals to action.

Be An Effective Word User, An Effective Communicator.

Quick Tips To Improve Communication.

We all have a system of preferences that we communicate within. Knowing another person's communication preference will allow you to speak with the person using their preferred system. Some people talk using kinaesthetic, others visual, some auditory or a mixture of all. For many years, this has been a technique businesses have used to sell products to us; through their words, pictures and smells, businesses influence us to buy products, without us even being aware at times.

So how does it work? For example, a person who communicates using kinaesthetic would make statements like "The sun really felt warm on my skin to day", "that doesn't feel right, that had an impact on me; I was moved by what you said".

Whereas a visual communicator statement would be "I get the picture, I see what you mean" While an auditory communicator statement would be something such as, "I hear what you are saying, that sounds good", "listen to the sounds of the birds". Auditory communicators are very good listeners, so be mindful of what you are saying, tone of voice is very important, especially to those whose preferred communication is auditory.

Remember, effective communication is key to building strong, lasting personal relationships. Next time you talk to someone, listen out for their preferred system and see what you learn. You may just find that you are more successful in achieving an outcome with a young person simply by understanding their preference and talking to them in that way.

#Speakingthesamelanguage

#Modelling

Tool 3 - Be Inspirational To Others, By Modelling Good Examples.

Children and young people learn from what they see around them. They model what they see on TV, the gangster rap that they listen to, they copy. We all copy to some degree, whether it is the clothes we wear, following the colours of the season, we are all influenced. Celebrities tend to be many individuals' choice of role models; we also have a generation of young people who look up to the 'road man', the top drug dealer, as a person to aspire to be like. Evident from the interviews I conducted, was the need for more positive role models within our communities. It is time for making the role models in our community more visible; the unsung heroes, it is their time to shine.

It may be hard to see the possibilities, when no one around you has achieved; if all a person sees is failure most of the time, what is the likelihood that individuals will aspire to want or expect more for their life? A child learns more from what they see than from what they are told. Parents teach a child how to look after money, for example, by the way they look after money. They learn how to handle situations by watching how others in the home handle situations. Many children are a reflection of their parents or the people that they surround themselves with the most.

Coming from a Council estate, single parent family, having dyslexia and running my own charity for over 10 years, has inspired others to believe that they too can achieve whatever they put their minds to. Those before us set the path which allows us to see what we can achieve, what is possible and beyond.

Imagine young people being exposed intentionally to role models and positive environments, the difference it would make. You do not have to sign up to be a role model, if you did not know already, you are a role model; your life speaks to people, you just may not be aware of this fact. Send out a message of hope, a message that inspires, a message that anything is possible, by the way that you live and conduct your life.

#LifeSkills

Tool 4 – PSHE: The Benefits Of Teaching Life Skills.

There are actions and there are outcomes; there are fruits and there are roots. Nurturing emotional well-being is important for young people to learn. Insecurity is evident in our society but how do you deal with it, where do you learn? Many seek external factors such as people, possessions and status to validate who they are. "Likes" on social media for some, makes them feel that they are worthwhile.

Educating young people from primary school age, about different concepts and tools through discussions and workshops, are necessary to prepare young people. Workshops can be delivered in the following areas:

- Enterprise – Many young people want to make money, so it is important to educate them how to make money for the long term, in a positive way.

- Self-worth and self-esteem, supporting young people to understand about loving themselves, valuing themselves and developing their confidence. Sexual Health - Inappropriate touching, bodily changes, Sexually Transmitted Infections, how to be assertive and healthy relationships.

- Life skills sessions, such as: cooking, money management, interpersonal skills and how to look after themselves.

- Drugs workshops, peer pressure, healthy living, leadership.

- How to develop Resiliences, which is fundamentally important to teach children and young people.

Emotional well-being, mixed with life skills sessions would be a very good topic to have as part of the school curriculum. Research over the years has made correlations between wellbeing and educational achievement, so in the long run investment in personal development in schools evidently could lead to better educational achievements. It is a win-win situation for all.

The great thing about this approach is that teachers can still focus upon what they do best, which is to teach and schools can use outside organisations, who are always willing to go into schools to deliver sessions on a variety of topics to support their students around life skills and emotional well-being, for example. It has been said that knowledge is power, whilst applied knowledge is powerful. Let us work together with teachers to provide young people with the right foundations, so that they can produce amazing fruits from their tree of life.

#Mentoring.

Tool 5 - Mentoring And Guidance: We All Need Support From Time To Time.

Mentoring was seen as an effective way of giving young people a voice, supporting them, alongside offering them the opportunity to be accountable. In the corporate environment, leaders have mentors, sponsors or coaches to aid with their development, we all could do with someone to help us along the way, right? Mentoring is effective in the business world and for people in general. I attend seminars, workshops and have developed a passion for reading. Most self helps books I have read, if not all, advise readers about the benefits of having mentoring - someone who can show you the way.

The internet gives us access to millions of people, that we can learn from.

Zig Ziglar says "You can have everything in life you want, if you will just help other people get what they want". Giving a young person a little attention and time can make a big difference. I am no longer surprised that simply remembering a young person's birthday can mean the world to them. "Miss, you remembered my birthday!". All young people should have a mentor whilst at school as we all have things that we would like to 'get off our chest' and having the opportunity, even if one does not use it, is a great resource

Guidance can be provided through mentoring; one reason given for why young people and children do not reach their full potential, was due to lack of guidance. Parents are the first people to provide direction. At all stages of life we need guidance, when working our way through the world at a young age, we need to learn from those around us who have the knowledge and experience to teach us. Remember you are a guide, providing direction and understanding to others and your input is needed. How much time are you willing to give on a monthly basis?

#Attitude

Tool 6 - The Difference Positive Attitude Can Make.

"You cannot tailor-make the situations in life, but you can tailor-make attitudes to fit the situation" Zig Ziglar

It is a person's attitude that will determine where he or she will go in life. Developing a positive attitude is not something that I learned or was taught how to develop at school. Not achieving potential in life is sometimes down to a person's attitude, not always their ability. Those with a positive attitude are likely to find the positives in almost every situation. People with a positive attitude will face problems too, just like everybody else but are more likely not to see a problem as a full stop.

Using Zig Ziglar's formula for developing a positive attitude, the following can be used with young people.

Step 1: Teaching young people that they have a choice; they can choose how they will react or respond to a situation, the power is in their hands. Exercise – Come up with 10-15 situations that young people could face and discuss their responses, looking at alternative responses to situations and their outcomes.

Step 2: Teaching and instilling the belief that anything is possible.

Visualising Exercises – In small groups, get the young people to visualise their dreams, telling them to dream as big as their minds will allow, they can have their eyes open or closed. This exercise opens the minds to a new way of thinking, painting pictures in the mind. It is said, "Seeing is believing". You have to believe that something can be done, in order to start making steps toward it and to continue in the face of adversity.

Step 3: Zig Ziglar believes that your hope for a better future, rather than your present, will be reflected in your attitude and so will affect your choices. There are many young people that lack belief for a better future. Many hold the mindset that only a select few are chosen to have a good future. Together let us support young people in developing and then holding a picture of a brighter future than their current situation. Exposing young people to others who have started where they are but were able to overcome challenges and make a difference in their life, encourages young people to start thinking about their own future in a more positive way, knowing that anything is possible.

#YourTime

Tool 7- Taking The Time To Just Be There.

Countless times I have heard young people, when having a heart to heart, express that people are not there for them. Being there for a young person no matter what, makes a difference. Being the person that a young person can turn to for help, makes a difference; having the tools, experience and knowledge to be able to help a young person makes a difference. It is not always the big actions that makes the difference, sometimes it is the small, daily actions that makes the biggest difference in a young person's life.

#Opportunities.

Tool 8 - Take Me Out Of My Comfort Zone And Expand My Thinking.

Have you ever read an autobiography or watched a TV show, where you have heard the words along the lines of 'If it were not for the opportunities that person X offered, I would not have been where I am today'? Opportunities are all around us. As Mario Testino said, "My favourite words are possibilities, opportunities and curiosity. I think if you are curious, you create opportunities, and then if you open the doors, you create possibilities". Opportunities open doors; one of the best experiences I have been able to offer 20 young people was to go to the French Alps. Taking a young person out of their environment offers so many benefits. Try it, take a group of young people for a long drive out of their surroundings and expand their minds through the things that they see. I do not know what it is but there is something impactful about taking young people out of their comfort zone, out of the same places that they see on a daily basis.

#Partnership

Tool 9 - Together We Can Make A Change.

Holistic ways of working are more effective and have greater impact. Schools, youth provision, police and parents all working together aids with keeping a close supportive eye on a young person. Working in isolation is not effective; a professional could be doing great work with a young person but if this learning is not mirrored at home or amongst friends, the learning can be lost. If you want to learn how to speak a new language, you would be more fully integrated into learning if you spent more time with indigenous people, right?

If you work with parents, you can identify needs together, support to offer at home; when you have school involvement, you can find out issues in school and they can find out about outside concerns and when working with the police, they may have concerns too, learning that you can share with each other, enabling all those involved to put a better support system in place.

#TimeForAction

Tool 10 – Action: What Will You Do From Today To Help One Young Person To Reach Their Full Potential?

1.

2.

3.

4.

5.

Thank you for reading this book, I hope that it has offered you insight into effective ways of working with children and young people, in order to help them to reach their full potential. It would take more than these pages to document all of the ways to help young people but in this book, I have made a start by highlighting some of the best H.E.L.P.

This is a start to inspire, stir up and to encourage people to keep on pushing to ensure that a change, one day soon, will come for our youth. In the world we live, having tenacity, commitment, love, care for others, passion, drive, empathy, patience and resilience, together we can turn around the lives of those deemed to be 'hard to reach', broken youth, those suffering and in need of help. It may appear far-fetched but once achieved, it will surely be a great miracle to see a dream for all children and young people reach their full potential, to become a reality.

Change is happening, let us not forget that; it may take one young person at a time but as long as we are on track for change, that is all that matters. Remember that your presence and smile will make a big difference. Never forget to show up and be the difference maker you are. Thank you once again, for investing your time to read 'The best H.E.L.P. Book'.

#TheBestH.E.L.P.Book

REFERENCES

Books:

Brian Tracy 'No Excuses - The Power of Self Discipline.'

Darren Hardy 'The Compound Effect: Jumpstart Your Income, Your Life, Your Success.'

Dr Stephen Covey ' 7 Habits Of Highly Effective People

Erik Erikson 'Youth and crisis'

Greg S. Reid and Sharon Lechter 'Three Feet from Gold: Turn Your Obstacles in Opportunities (Think and Grow Rich).'

James Allen 'As a Man Thinketh.'

Jeffs and Smith 2010 'Youth Work Practice.'

John C. Coleman and Leo B. Hendry 'The Nature of Adolescence.' John Maxwell, 'Today Matters - 12 daily Practices to guarantee tomorrow's success.'

John Maxwell '25 Ways To Win With People; How to Make Others Feel Like a Million Bucks.'

Joyce Meyer 'Approval Addiction: Overcoming Your Need to Please Everyone.' Sue Knight 'NLP at work'

Susan Jeffers 'Feel the Fear and Do It Anyway.'

Wayne Allyn 'RootsThe Joy Of Failure; How To Turn Failure, Rejection And Pain Into Extraordinary Success.'

Journals:

Colin Brent 'Lost in the middle: Reappraising the role of the youth centre in youth work provision.' (http://www.youthpolicy.org/blog/youth-work-community-work/lost-in-themiddle-reappraising-the-role-of-theyouth-centre/)

DrMylesMunroehttps://www.youtube.com/watch?v=VG2OsRyzN4Q

Long beach California dress code research - http://www.enotes.com/researchstarters/dress-codes-uniformspublic-schools

Types of Parenting Styles 'Learn How Each Parenting Style Impacts Children' By Amy Morin, LCSW Updated June 21, 2016; 2 https://www.verywell.com/types-ofparenting-styles-1095045

David M. Fergusson, L. John Horwood, Elizabeth M. Ridder (2004), 'Show me the child at seven: the consequences of conduct problems in childhood for psychosocial functioning in adulthood' (Journal of Child Psychology and Psychiatry)

Dr. Blaslotto at the University of Chicago; 'Study on skills throwing a basketball.'

Eliza Martinez on 'The Effects of Bad Parenting on Children.'http://oureverydaylife.com/effectsbad-parenting-children-2995.html

Guardian Articles on funding cuts; https://www.theguardian.com/society 3 /2016/aug/10/teenagers-isolatedidle-youth-clubs-services-closed

http://www.youngminds.org.uk/- Figures On Mental Health

Mariana EizirikI; David Simon Bergmann; 'Father absence and its influence on child and adolescent development: a case report.' Rev. psiquiatr. Rio Gd. Sul vol.26 no.3 Porto Alegre Sept./Dec. 2004

Michael Young 'what is school for', http://www.fpce.up.pt/ciie/revistaesc/ ESC32/ESC32_Arquivo.pdf

National Youth Agency - Youth Services in England: The State of the Nation http://www.nya.org.uk/wpcontent/uploads/2014/06/YouthServices-in-England_-The-State-ofthe-Nation.pdf 4

Sir Alasdair Macdonald's report into PSHE http://www.educationengland.org.uk/ documents/pdfs/2009-macdonaldpshe.pdf

http://www.bibalex.org/search4dev/fil es/283337/115519.pdf ('A guide to promoting resilience in children: strengthening the human spirit' Edith Grotberg, Ph.D. The International Resilience Project Bernard van Leer Foundation)

Additional Reading:

Dr Andrew Dobson – 'Who am I? Self-Identity – How to Build Personal Character.'

Dr Phill http://www.ayph.org.uk/publications/ 480_KeyData2013_ WebVersion.pdf

http://www.infed.org/archives/usinginformaleducation/ jeffsandsmith1.htm

Mary Morse (Author) Children development institute https:// childdevelopmentinfo.com/

Maslow's 'Hierarchy of Needs.' https://m.simplypsychology.org/ maslow.html

People Interviewed who wanted to be named:

Arnold Oceng, Actor

Commissioning Officer for the Council,

Craig Whittaker MP

Dan Charlish Founder of Snow Camp

Derrick Anderson, Former Lambeth Chief Executive

Jaja Soze, founder of PDC Music label and Indigo Youth

Louise McNestrie, CEO of BeYOU Training

Marsha Powell, Founder of Believe UK,

Miss Tracey Donnelley, Manager Of Children's 3 Service At Young People Matter.

Mr Anthony Douglas, Consultant and Manager in the Music and Acting Industry

Mr Devon Hanson, Principal of Evelyn Grace Academy

Mr Gary Philips, Head Of Lilian Baylis School

Mr Opy Onas, Founder of Proten International

Mr Mark Scott, Manager of Life Skills Centre

Nicola Brookstein, Director of Caboodle Arts Company Ltd &

Caboodle Theatre in Education

Rachel Beckles, Former employee of 4children

Teresa Priest, Walcot Foundation

Tim Brown, CEO of Raw Material (Music and the arts programme for young people)

Toni Harriott, St Giles Trust SOS project

Trayvon Edwards, young person

People quoted throughout the book:

Albert Einstein

Blaise Pascal

Buddha

Charles R Swindoll

Dalai Lama

David Cameron

Dr Myles Munroe

Erich Fromm

Franklin D Roosevelt

George Bernard Shaw

George Elliot

Grenville Kleiser

Helen Keller

Henry Ford

James Russell Lowell

Jim Rohn

Joel Scott Osteen

Johann Wolfgang von Goethe

John McDonnell

Les Brown Mahatma Gandhi

Mario Testino

Mark Caine

Mark Twain

Martin Luther King, Jr.

Mary McLeod Bethune

Mathew l Jacobson

Mickey Rooney

Muhammad Yunus

Napoleon Hill Author

Nelson Mandela

Oscar Wilde

Princess Diana

Steven Davis

The New King James Bible

TD Jakes

Zig Ziglar

People and funders named throughout the book:

Adolf Hitler

All Girls Rock

Barack Obama

Charles Darrow

Chris Gardner

Howard Schultz

J.K. Rowling

Joanna Oliver

Jenni Steels foundation

Juvenis youth

Karl- Lokko,

Kids Company

Michael Jordon

Mr Marcus Dawes

Ms Ookolo

Oprah Winfrey

Self-Empowerment for Life foundation

Tony Robbins

Tolu Oyerunda

Young Mums Support Network

Funders Named

City Bridge Trust

Four Acre Trust

St James's place

Walcot Foundation

RESOURCES

PROMOTING RESILIENCE IN CHILDREN:

Resilience is the capacity to face, overcome and even be transformed by adversity. Edith Grotberg conducted research into developing resilience in children, her work is titled "A guide to promoting resilience in children: strengthening the human spirit". This is a useful guide for a clear understanding about a range of resiliences and how to support children to develop them. Presented on page 33 of this document, there are useful activities which can be used with young people.

Below I have included a link to this document:

http://bibalex.org/baifa/Attachment/Documents/115519.pdf

If sourcing via a search engine, type in the name of the research 'A guide to promoting resilience in children: strengthening the human spirit', to access the document.

An Activity taken from the document – Discussion on Resilience.

Step 1 - List on a board or paper some of the adversities people face in our society. If the group is small enough and comfortable enough to participate, ask the participants to indicate some of the adversities they know about or have experienced. (This can also be done when working with individuals). Then discuss some of the ways to deal with adverse situations listed.

Step 2 - Discuss 'I AM' resilience factors.

Make clear that I AM factors are feelings, attitudes, beliefs and strengths within a child. These are what stay with a child all of his or her life. They can be strengthened by support. Encourage them to describe personal experiences in fostering I AM resilience factors.

For example: I am lovable, I am proud of myself, I am responsible, I am hopeful for my future, I am trust worthy.

Step 3 - Discuss 'I CAN' resilience factors. Explain to the group that these are social and interpersonal skills children learn and acquire and are tools for interacting with other people which must be taught and learned. Have the group discuss social and interpersonal skills they have learned, or have seen in other children.

For example: I can communicate, I can problem solve and I can seek trusting relationships.

Step 4 - Discuss 'I HAVE' resilience factors, which are the support, resources and external help that is available to participants. Have the group discuss the support children know they have and the resources available in a family and community. Encourage participants to describe how they can use their family and community support and resources.

For example: I have trusting relationships, I have access to education, I have a loving family and I have role models in my community and my home. Have the group discuss inner strengths they have seen in children and what can be done to help promote these inner strengths.

Step 5 - Put the 'I HAVE, I AM, I CAN' resilience factors in a dynamic relationship with each other. Discuss how these factors work in a dynamic way together. Some guiding questions to help the discussion might be:

1. If the parent or other adult protects the child from all adversities, can the child strengthen his/her sense of autonomy, control and responsibility?

2. If the adult speaks for the child in a conflict with another child, can the child learn a social skill, like negotiation?

3. If the child does things independently without help or advice from adults, is he or she at greater risk of harm or failure?

4. How do these dynamics change with age? How are these dynamics influenced by individual differences?

This is just a snapshot, to enable you to think about how you can start introducing the concept of resilience to children and young people, please refer to the link for more in-depth understanding of the activity presented above.

'CLEAN QUESTIONING' USING COACHING SKILLS

Communication is part of our everyday lives and communicating effectively offers many benefits. In Neuro Linguistic Programming (NLP) and coaching, there is a concept referred to as, 'clean language', it is very simple to learn with practice and will definitely increase an individual's communication skills. So, what is clean language? Sue Knight described it as being "native, present, open, not knowing, alert, aware, fascinated, eager to learn and selfless".

Take a moment to think about the last time a young person or a friend came to you to discuss an issue. Now ask yourself:

- Where was your attention when they were speaking?

- Were you listening?

- Were you thinking about what you were going to say next?

Often when communicating with others, it is quite usual to answer without really listening. A young person comes to you with a concern, for example around being in a gang, issue with friends, parents, teacher or about a breakdown in a relationship with their boyfriend or girlfriend. Do you often already have the answer for them, as you have heard a similar story before? You have a solution to suggest based upon your experience and knowledge, right?

This could mean that you are imposing your map of the world onto another person, yet everyone will experience and process the same situation differently. I have found from my experience, that many people spend most of their time suggesting solutions, rather than listening for understanding and that very few people use clean language, when supporting a person.

So how can you use clean language? There are key questions which may be asked when communicating with an individual, to assist with listening and to ensure that you are using clean language, as shown in this example:

(The above diagram link: http://www.cleanlanguage.co.uk/
articles/articles/109/1/Less-Is-More-The-Art-of-Clean-Language/
Page1.html**)**

CLEAN QUESTIONING IN ACTION

Young Person: I felt I was making very good progress.

Worker: You were making progress in what way?

Young Person: I was not getting in trouble.

Worker: Not getting in trouble, what do you mean?

Young Person: Well I was going to school and coming home on time.

Worker: When you were going to school and coming home on time, what did that mean to you?

Young Person: Hmmm, it meant I was making my parents happy.

The example above demonstrates the worker repeating back what has been said and asking questions to gain a better understanding of what 'progress' meant to the young person. An unclean question would have been:

Worker: So you are not making progress anymore because you're misbehaving again?

Or are you not doing well at school?

The young person has not explained what 'not making progress' means. The worker's reply would imply that he or she already knows why the young person is not making progress, without knowing what progress means to the individual. Can you think back to the last conversation you had with a young person?

1. Did you come up with a conclusion to what was being said before they had told you the full story?

2. Did you use your own representation of the world to understand what they were saying?

3. Did you listen fully to what was being said?

Clean questions support the way that you can relate with a young person because you are using their words and trying to find out what things mean to them instead of coming up with your own interpretation from what is being said. Clean questioning can help a person to find the answer to their problem themselves, simply by you asking questions that lead an individual to think. The answers to our problems lay within us already, we just have to be willing to search for them. Give it a try the next time you are talking with a young person. Ask questions instead of giving advice and allow the young person to come up with the answers for themselves.

AN EXAMPLE OF A FUNDER'S FEEDBACK FORM

Feedback is an effective way for another person or organisation to evaluate areas for improvement. Below is an example of a form that funders could use to give feedback to applicants.

Name of Organisation:	Date:	✔
Overall Feedback:		
Areas of Improvement	*Tick if areas needs to be improved* *(More in-depth form could identify what needs to be improved)*	
Governance and Documents	Missing documents. Governance Structures not in place. Other	
Budget	Figures do not add up. Not cost effective. Figures are not realistic. Other	
Project	Similar project in the area. Does not demonstrate what you are going to do. Not very clear.	
Outcomes	Outcomes are not clear. Not cost effective. Outcomes do not match outputs.	
Need For The Project	The need for the project is not clearly demonstrated. Does not demonstrate needs in your area. More research or evidence needed.	
Milestones	No clear steps for achieving the outcomes.	
Sustainability Of Project	No sustainability plan for the future. Project is not sustainable.	
Track Record Of Organisation	New organisation with no track record. New project with no evidence of achievement.	
Partnership Work	Other groups delivering similar programmes in the area. Project should be delivered in partnership.	

GOAL SETTING WORK SHEET

Darren Hardy is a reputable source for excellent goal setting tools, many of which may be found on his website: www.TheCompoundEffect.com

Goal setting allows an individual to think about what they want to achieve, the how, the why and the when. In the exercise below, think about goals that you would like to achieve in the different areas and then write them down. The 'why' you want a particular goal is important because when the going gets tough, the 'why', will keep you going. Helping young people to come up with a plan for their future is really useful, in getting them to think about more than where they currently are. Please note, a young person does not have to make goals in all the areas below but areas that they feel that they would like to focus on.

Area Of Goals	State what you want to achieve and why?	Steps to achieving your desired goal.	Support Needed	Time Frame
Business/Career				
Family Life				
Financial				
Health and well being				
Family				
Spiritual				
Relationships and social				

'QUALITIES, TALENTS AND KNOWLEDGE' WORKSHEET

Instruction:

1. Give each young person a piece of paper, then ask them to make a list of their skills, qualities and talents.

2. Afterwards, hand them the list of qualities below, this may aid them with adding to their list (you may find the young people find it hard to list good things about themselves).

3. Next, encourage the young people to read their list to the rest of the group.

4. Finally, explain to the young people, the benefits of the activity that they have just completed. Encourage them to take their paper home and to refer to it any time that they need a reminder of how great they are.

Sincere	Considerate	Broad-Minded	Good reader
Understanding	Good-Natured	Gentle	Good at doing hair
Loyal	Reliable	Well-Spoken	Compassionate
Truthful	Mature	Educated	Independent
Trustworthy	Earnest	Reasonable	Knowledgeable
Intelligent	Kind	Companionable	Inspiring
Dependable	Friendly	Likeable	Visionary
Open-Minded	Kind-Hearted	Trusting	Problem Solver
Thoughtful	I am Happy	Clever	Open Handed
Wise	Sociable	Pleasant	Merciful
Honest	Charming	Imaginative	Encouraging
Entertaining	Humble	Forgiving	Good Singer
Adventurous	Tidy	Helpful	Good at Football
Vivacious	Popular	Outstanding	Compassionate
Composed	Practical	Self-Disciplined	Problem Solver
Relaxed	Light-Hearted	Enthusiastic	Artistic
Romantic	Punctual	Polite	Comprehensive
Proficient	Creative	Ambitious	Neutral
Rational	Interesting	Well-Mannered	Passionate
Skilful	Good-Humoured	Energetic	Amicable
Enterprising	Responsible	Easy-going	Intuitive
Gracious	Cheerful	Spotty	Considerate
Able	Trustful	Good at creative art	forward-thinking
Nice	Warm-Hearted	supportive	quick learner
Agreeable	Self-Confident	Friendly	Helpful
Productive	Strong-Minded	Knowledgeable	Special

FUNDING BODIES

Please see below, links to websites to access information about sources of funding and a list of funding bodies you can apply to.

The Henry Smith Charity	The JA Trust	The William P Bancroft Charitable Foundation
The Blandford Lake Trust	The Jomati Foundation	The Wingate Charitable Trust
The Brillig Charitable Trust	The Livingstone Trust	The Allan and Nesta Ferguson Charitable Trust
St James Place	The Man Group plc. Charitable Trust	The Barbara Ward Children's Foundation
The Compton Foundation	Matrix Chambers Fund	The BEARR Trust
The Adamson Trust	City Bridge	The Bryan Guinness Charitable Trust
The Dulverton Trust	Mercers Foundation	The Constance Green Foundation
The Eleanor Rathbone Trust	The Mustard Seed Trust	The Elena Trust
Esmee Fairbairn Foundation	The Nando Peretti Foundation	CMCK Foundation
The Evan Cornish Charitable Trust	LTSB Foundation	The Fulmer Charitable Trust
The Wakeham Trust	Cicely Northcate trust	Hope for Children
Peter Mint Trust	The Polden Puckham Charitable Foundation	Ian Mactaggart Trust
Garfield Weston Foundation	Rhododendron Trust	Lord Michelham of Hellingly Foundation
The Gibbs Charitable Trust	Rockefeller Brothers Foundation	Radley Charitable Trust
The Haramead Trust	The Rowan Charitable Foundation	The Ashworth Charitable Trust
The Hilden Charitable Fund	The Samuel Rubin Charitable Foundation	The Souter Foundation
The Hinchley Charitable Trust	The Schmidt Family Foundation	The Trusthouse Charitable Foundation
Humanity United	The Scott Bader Foundation	The Serve All Trust
Co operative	Awards for All	The Stanley Thomas Johnson Trust
Peabody	London Community Foundation	Wates Foundation

WEBSITE LINKS TO ACCESS FOR FUNDING

www.firesouls.co.uk

www.idoxopen4community.co.uk/worcestershire

http://www.fundingcentral.org.uk

http://www.lotterygoodcauses.org.uk /funding-finder

http://www.governmentfunding.org.uk

MASLOW HIERARCHY OF NEEDS

Maslow's hierarchy of needs was developed many years ago. Maslow found from his research as a Humanistic Psychologist, that there are general patterns of human needs, which follow the same sequence. From his work, he was able to highlight that each level needs to be achieved before a person can move onto the next level. As humans, we all have needs that we are seeking to be met, understanding these needs, can aid us with supporting a child or young person to meet these needs where possible.

NOTES: